FAITH AND REASON

I enjoy sharing my books as I do my friends, asking only that you treat them well and see them safely home

The Lake of Galilee

FAITH
AND
REASON
A FIRST COURSE IN
APOLOGETICS

BY

AUSTIN G. SCHMIDT, S. J.
PROFESSOR OF EDUCATION
LOYOLA UNIVERSITY, CHICAGO

AND

JOSEPH A. PERKINS, A. M.
ASSISTANT PROFESSOR OF PHILOSOPHY
LOYOLA UNIVERSITY, CHICAGO

SECOND AND REVISED EDITION

LOYOLA UNIVERSITY PRESS
CHICAGO, ILLINOIS
1937

Imprimi Potest:

> G. A. FITZGIBBONS, S. J.
> > *Provincial of the Chicago Province*

August 9, 1937

Imprimatur:

> ✠ GEORGE CARDINAL MUNDELEIN
> > *Archbishop of Chicago*

August 11, 1937

PREFACE TO THE SECOND EDITION

IN PREPARING this revised edition, the authors made full use of all suggestions received since the first appearance of this work. The illustrations were completely remade. Chapters I, VII, IX, and XV were rewritten more fully, but without material changes in the original draft. Chapter XXX was combined with Chapter XXXI. The remaining chapters have but a few scattered changes.

It is hoped that in its new form the book will continue to exercise a helpful influence in developing an intelligent grasp of the facts which prove the essential harmony existing between faith and reason.

A. G. S.
J. A. P.

TABLE OF CONTENTS

FAITH AND REASON

CHAPTER ONE

THE PURPOSE OF THE BOOK

HE MEANING OF APOLOGETICS. We are accustomed to think of an *apology* as an expression of regret for something of which we are ashamed. But the word in its first meaning signifies an *explanation.* Apologetics, then, is a theological science which has for its object the explanation and defense of Christianity as taught by the Catholic Church. The other branches of theology—dogmatic, moral, and ascetical—assume that we are members of the Catholic Church who are prepared to accept her teachings. Hence dogmatic theology sets forth what we must *believe,* moral theology tells us how we must *act,* and ascetical theology explains how to *arrive at perfection* in imitation of Christ and the saints, but all without proving that the Catholic Church has the right to teach with authority on these important subjects. Apologetics, on the other hand, goes to the very foundation and gives the proofs for the fact that the

claims of the Catholic Church are reasonable. It provides a scientific vindication of the grounds for believing in the Catholic religion. It shows that our faith is trustworthy. It answers the question: Why should I be a Catholic?

After one has become a Catholic, he accepts that faith which the Catholic Church, guided and protected by the Holy Spirit, proposes to him as true. But his own reason must first convince him that the claims of the Church are worthy of his acceptance. Christ Himself did not ask men to join His standard without making it possible for them to perceive through the use of their reason that they ought to do so. He appealed to the uprightness of His life, the truth of His doctrine, and above all to the miracles which He wrought, as evidence of His Messiahship. Hence this book is called FAITH AND REASON because it shows how through the use of reason we can arrive at the certainty that the claims of the Catholic Church are true.

We who were born Catholics do not take up this study because we have begun to doubt what our faith teaches. We study apologetics for two very good purposes:

The first is in order to be prepared to answer the questions and difficulties of honest inquirers. True, a person who has become seriously interested in the Catholic religion should be sent to a priest for instruction, but before he reaches this stage he has very probably been influenced by the intelligent knowledge of their religion shown by Catholic friends and acquaintances.

The second purpose is to protect our own faith in every way possible. We are not living in a secluded community where everyone is a Catholic and where the teachings of the Church are accepted without question. We are living in a world where two opposing forces, those of Catholicism and of rationalism, are in constant conflict. Very probably we have already heard sneers, doubts, denials, and counter arguments. We shall hear more of them. There is of course a great deal of good in the world. There are many God-fearing persons, both Catholics and non-Catholics. But there are also tremendous forces working for evil, and these forces are often hostile to the Catholic Church because she stands so resolutely for the old truths which they deny. Let us mention some of the conditions which make it more necessary for every Catholic to understand the arguments for his faith:

1. Millions of persons have no belief in God, and there are in many countries societies for the promotion of atheism. In our own country, not long ago, when a group of Protestant clergymen were asked to state whether they believed in a personal God, some said that they did not. If clergymen have such ideas, what must we expect of others?

2. Outside the Catholic Church, many of those who profess to be Christians do not believe that Jesus Christ was truly God, and many are not even certain that He ever existed.

3. There is a great exaggeration of the importance of science, and you will hear and read many things to the effect that only science can be depended upon as true and that the things taught by religion are only myths and legends.

4. The governments of the world go from one extreme

to another in regard to social justice. Sometimes they encourage a capitalism which makes it possible for a few men to acquire enormous fortunes to the injury of the common people, and at other times they put into effect a communistic system which destroys private ownership entirely. The true and solid principles of social justice as laid down by Christ are seldom perfectly understood and applied.

5. There is great laxity in regard to marriage and holy purity. Divorce is most common. Free love, companionate marriage, and birth control are openly advocated. Old safeguards of purity have been cast aside.

6. The great agencies of education, communication, and recreation—the state universities, the press, the radio, and the movies—have for the most part no religious convictions. God has a very small place in the world which they create.

7. Finally—this is not a force working for evil, but we may mention it in this connection—the people among whom you will live are better educated than people used to be. If you are to exert on non-Catholics the fullest possible influence, you also should be well educated.

WHAT FACTS NEED PROOFS? The science of apologetics provides proofs for all those things that must be accepted if one is to believe in the claims of the Catholic Church. What proofs need to be stressed will depend upon the times. St. Peter became the first Christian apologist when on Pentecost Day he stood before the Jews and demonstrated the divinity of Christ from the testimony of the prophets and from Christ's resurrection. These were the things that needed proof if he was to convince the Jews of

Prejudiced scholarship . . . armed power . . . and ignorance . . . these are the three forces which the Christian apologist of the day must be prepared to meet.

his day. The *Apology* of St. Justin the Martyr, written in 150, the *Plea for the Christians* of Athenagoras, written in 177, and the *Three Books of Evidences against the Jews* of St. Cyprian, written in 250, emphasized the points necessary to answer the difficulties of the followers of Roman paganism. Then for some centuries the efforts of the apologists were directed against the Mohammedans. Later the apologists of the Church wrote with particular reference to the teachings of Luther, Calvin, Huss, and Wickliff. All these apologists could safely assume that God exists. But today we cannot even take it for granted that our adversaries will admit this much. If we begin by attempting to prove that Christ was the Messias sent by God, we may find that our opponent denies the existence of God altogether. If we affirm that the Catholic religion is the one by means of which we can save our souls, we may be met with the statement that we have no souls to save. Hence the Catholic apologist of today must go to the very bed rock and establish each one of the following propositions:

1. That a Creator exists.
2. That this Creator is an infinite, omnipotent, eternal, wise, and good God.
3. That every man has a soul which is spiritual and immortal.
4. That every man has an obligation of practising religion.
5. That a purely natural religion is not sufficient to meet man's needs.
6. That God can reveal supernatural truths to men and that in fact He did reveal certain ones.
7. That a great and unchangeable revelation was made through Jesus Christ.
8. That Jesus Christ was both God and man.

9. That Jesus Christ established a Church with perpetual authority to teach with infallible certitude His doctrines and to administer His sacraments.

10. That God desires all men to avoid sin, to lead supernatural lives, and to save their souls by becoming faithful members of the Catholic Church.

YOUR TASK AS AN APOLOGIST. You already know and accept these facts. But it is one thing to know a fact, and it is another thing to know the *proof*, or the *reason*, or the *explanation* for a fact.

Even little children know what the Catholic Church teaches, and know that what she teaches is true. For since Christ came to save all men, and to save them through His Church, He did not institute a Church of such a kind that only a highly educated person could recognize it as His Church.

In His infinite wisdom and goodness He brought into existence, and has kept in existence, a Church which even simple and uneducated people can see is the true Church. The Church, in the beauty and completeness of her doctrine, in her wonderful worship, in her calm and unwavering adherence to fixed principles, in her holiness as manifested in the lives of her saints, in her unlikeness to other churches, which say one thing today and a contradictory thing tomorrow, is a sufficient proof of her own divine foundation. John L. Stoddard, famous American lecturer, lived for many years as an agnostic—that is, as one who believes that man's mind can arrive at nothing certain concerning God and religion. Late in life he entered the Catholic Church, and there he found complete rest for his mind. The following are some

[7]

of the stanzas in a poem which he wrote shortly after his first Communion:

> Time-hallowed Church, whose truth divine
> Endures unchanged from age to age,
> What joy to feel that we are thine,
> Nor lost our precious heritage!
>
> How sweet now to devoutly kneel
> Where oft our feet so lightly trod,
> And in her lamp-lit shrines to feel
> The presence of the Son of God!
>
> Dear Mother Church, with grateful tears
> We find the blessed fold of Rome,
> Sad from the long past's wasted years,
> But thankful to have reached our home.

Every good Catholic knows, and feels, and is convinced that the Church is his true home. God is there. Jesus is there in the Blessed Sacrament. Our Mother Mary is there. The angels are there. All the means of grace are there. Compared with this, what any other church has to offer is nothing but emptiness, uncertainty, and confusion. We know this. We have sufficient proof for it. Our purpose now is not to learn proofs for the first time, but to take all our proofs and organize them—systematize them—go down to the very foundation on which they rest. In our education up to this point the emphasis was on *what* the Church teaches. Now the emphasis is to be on the *arguments for the truth of what she teaches.* The old foundation was sufficient, but the new one will be far deeper.

ADVANTAGES OF A DEEPER KNOWLEDGE.

Some of the advantages of having a full, complete knowledge of the reasons behind our faith are these:

1. This knowledge helps toward giving us a greater firmness in our faith.

2. This knowledge makes us appreciate better the beauty and grandeur of our faith, which is the one perfectly true and consistent body of spiritual truth in a world full of follies and confusion.

3. The effort to arrive at this knowledge, requiring as it does clear and careful thinking, is an excellent training for the mind.

4. One who understands his faith can do much more than others to assist those who are seeking the truth. He can answer questions and give proofs. All good Catholics teach others by word and example, but those who know the most can teach the most.

POINTS FOR REVIEW AND DISCUSSION

1. In his book entitled *The Fairest Argument,* Bishop John F. Noll quotes the following statements from Protestant clergymen and scholars, most of whom have died since writing these passages. On pages 6 and 7 we mentioned ten facts concerning which we need to have proofs. Which of these facts is contradicted by each of the following statements?

    a. "A precise theory of the origin of the universe and of man and sin is surely no essential part of the Christian faith" (Rev. George Jackson, Methodist, Toronto, Canada).

    b. "The Bible is not connected with twentieth-century life.

We should make our own Christianity for our own age" (Professor Votaw, University of Chicago).

c. "It has been said that Jesus Christ was God, but no New Testament writer has said so. You get that idea from the creeds made by men. Nor is there any reference to the Trinity in the New Testament. Mark, John, Luke, and Paul say nothing about Jesus having come into the world in a miraculous way" (Rev. Charles F. Aked, Baptist, San Francisco).

2. Lord Macaulay, great English essayist, paid the following tribute to the Catholic Church:

"She saw the commencement of all the governments and all the ecclesiastical establishments that now exist in the world; and we have no assurance that she is not destined to see the end of them all. She was great and respected before the Saxon set foot on Britain, before the Frank had passed the Rhine, when Grecian eloquence still flourished in Antioch, when idols were still worshipped in the temple of Mecca. And she may still exist in undiminished vigor when some traveler from New Zealand shall, in the midst of a vast solitude, take his stand on a broken arch of London Bridge, to sketch the ruins of St. Paul's."

Lord Macaulay believed these things, and yet he never became a Catholic. Let the class discuss this matter, and put down in order the truths of which we would have to convince a man like Lord Macaulay in order to convert him.

THE NEXT LESSON

After this introduction, the first thing we wish to prove is that God exists. There are various arguments for His existence, one of which is based upon the design or purpose which we see in the universe. This we will explain in the next lesson.

THE PROOF FROM DESIGN

ICERO'S TESTIMONY.
If you have studied Latin, you must have
read in class some of the speeches of
Cicero. This Roman orator, a pagan who
knew nothing about Christ, once said:
"When we look up at the sky, and contemplate the
heavenly bodies, can anything be more plain and obvious
than that there is some higher being of surpassing intelligence governing all these things?" (*De Natura Deorum,*
II, 2).

Not in the skies alone, but everywhere in the world, we
find a wonderful order and design which prove the existence
of a great Designer. Let us see why this is so.

DESIGN AND DESIGNER. No doubt you have a
radio set at home. A radio set consists of a wooden box
within which are numerous metal plates and coils, and one
or more glass tubes which give forth a faint light when the
set is in operation. By turning on and 'tuning in' the radio,

you are able to hear programs transmitted from great distances.

The radio is a delicate and complicated instrument. Everything in it has a purpose, and everything must be very carefully made and adjusted. If any part is defective or out of order, the radio will not operate satisfactorily.

When we see the order and design in the radio, and when we consider how it produces a certain effect, we know with certainty that *it did not just happen to be*. Somebody *made it*. Somebody *knew what he was doing* when he made it. Somebody *had a purpose* in making it.

What we say of the radio is true of innumerable other instruments and machines which man has made. Consider for a moment the automobile, the airplane, the microscope and the telescope, the camera, the electric refrigerator, the telephone, and thousands of other instruments or machines which you see, use, or read about every day. There are only two possible explanations for their existence. One is that pieces of wood, metal, and other materials *just happened* to become assembled as they are found to be assembled. It is impossible to believe this. For first of all, each single piece had to be of a certain shape—some round, some square, some of this size and thickness and some of that. Then all these pieces or parts had to come together with a certain order and arrangement. But it is impossible that they should ever do this of themselves. Imagine that you had all the parts of a radio lying separately on a bench. Would they in a million years gather themselves together to form the radio? Would they ever do so even if they were kept in continual motion, so that their chance of meeting in the proper position was increased?

Your common sense tells you that they would not. Nothing could ever convince you of the contrary. And therefore, since the first explanation—that the radio was the result of chance—is impossible and ridiculous, the only other possible explanation must be accepted: The radio was made by someone with intelligence who had a purpose in making it.

We can, therefore, formulate the principle: *Complicated order and design prove the existence of an intelligent designer.*

ORDER AND DESIGN IN NATURE.

But no instrument or machine made by man can ever equal in delicacy,

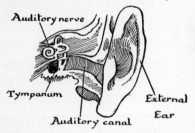

beauty, and efficiency the wonderful works of nature. We have on this page a diagram of the human ear, a far more wonderful thing than the costliest radio ever made. You see first of all the external ear, including the auditory canal, by means of which the sound vibrations in the air are carried to the tympanum, a membrane somewhat like the leather head of a drum. When the sound vibrations in the air reach the tympanum, it too is set vibrating. Beyond the tympanum is a complicated system of sacs and tubes, filled with a fluid, and through them the vibrations are carried to the end of the auditory nerve.

Nobody knows, and perhaps nobody ever will know, just how those vibrations are carried by the auditory nerve to the brain. And when they reach the brain—that marvelous mass of nerve cells and nerve fibers—they produce, in a way which we simply cannot understand, the sensation of sound. We carry about with us this compact and wonderful instrument, and through it we are able to hear and to distinguish between a thousand different sounds—the voices of friends, the songs of birds, the tones of musical instruments, and other sounds far too numerous to mention.

The radio is indeed a wonderful instrument. But what does the radio do? It merely captures and intensifies those vibrations in the air. But it does not give to human beings the power of hearing. No man has ever made a human ear. No man has ever done anything to restore a single one of the many parts of the ear after it has been destroyed.

In Holy Scripture we read the following story:

And they bring to Him one deaf and dumb; and they besought Him that He would lay His hand upon him. And taking him from the multitude apart, He put His fingers into his ears, and spitting, He touched his tongue. And looking up to heaven, He groaned, and said to him: "Ephpheta," which is, "Be thou opened." And immediately his ears were opened, and the string of his tongue was loosed, and he spoke right (Mark 7:32-35).

There are some irreligious men who do not believe this story. But there is no man, Catholic or non-Catholic, who would not say (unless prejudice caused him to reject the conclusions of his own intellect): "If this thing happened just as it is described, the One who did it is divine."

OTHER MARVELS OF NATURE. Did it ever occur to you to inquire why it is that we speak of 'Mother Earth'? What do we mean by 'earth,' and why do we call it 'mother'?

Go out to the fields and get a handful of earth. Hold it in your hand and look at it. It is dead, motionless. We call it 'dirty.' We do not usually look upon it as particularly useful.

But consider what this earth does. A seed falls upon it; the rain falls from heaven and moistens the earth; the seed begins to grow. The tiny roots draw up the nourishment found in the earth, and the plant converts this nourishment into its own substance. What was once earth (or in the earth) becomes wheat or corn. Animals and men eat the wheat or corn, and convert it into their own substance. There is no living thing—no tree, no flower, no animal, no man— that did not get all the matter in it from the earth. The fragrant rose was once earth. The lovely face of a little baby was once earth. We are correct when we speak of 'Mother Earth.' And when these living things die, whatever is material in them returns to the earth from which it came, and the endless process of birth and death is repeated generation after generation.

MARVELS OF THE HEAVENS. The great Catholic scientist Pasteur said that his faith grew stronger and deeper the more he knew of the marvels of nature. Pasteur did most of his work with the microscope, studying those invisible organisms which cause milk to sour, or wounds to become infected, or human beings to die when bitten by a mad dog. But if we turn from these microscopic organisms to the huge bodies which we see in the heavens, we find the same evidences of wisdom, design, and purpose. Few have expressed this idea more beautifully than John L. Stoddard in *Rebuilding a Lost Faith,* page 35:

In this vast, shoreless sea of space we,—earth-imprisoned voyagers,—find ourselves on the surface of a tiny satellite, whirling upon its axis at the rate of a thousand miles an hour. Although we feel no motion, not only are we turning thus, but are also being borne along our planet's path around the sun with a velocity of 1,080 miles a minute, or *one and a half million miles a day!* Moreover, in addition to all this, our entire solar system is sweeping onward through infinity at a rate of 400,000,000 miles a year, and entering thus continually new regions of sidereal space! Yet is there no appreciable danger of collision; for our solar colony, vast though its limits are, is but a point in a gigantic solitude. Our isolation is almost inconceivable. Our nearest astral neighbour moves at a distance of 275,000 times the earth's distance from the sun, which is itself 92,000,000 miles! Yet this star is exceptionally near!

And what *we* do in our small corner of the universe, millions of other suns and satellites are doing,—swinging in perfect equilibrium millions of miles from one another, and moving with such perfect regularity that most of their vast changes can be foretold to a minute centuries in advance, or ascertained at any date of the historic past!

Yet the same law that guides the motion of Arcturus regulates the falling leaf. The same Divine hand paints the sunset glory and the petals of the rose. Proofs of design and wisdom, which overpower one in his study of astronomy, are just as evident in every other sphere of science. The revelations of the microscope are as marvellous as those of the telescope. The same supreme Intelligence is discoverable in the infinitely small as in the infinitely great. The ornithologist finds an adaptation of means to ends in the wonderful structure of birds; the zoologist traces it in every form of animal life; the botanist is filled with reverence and admiration in his investigation of the fertilisation of flowers; the worker in the laboratory is lost in wonder at the mysteries of chemical affinities; and if "an undevout astronomer is mad," so also is an undevout investigator of the universe in any field of knowledge he may enter.

CHANCE CANNOT EXPLAIN ORDER. If all this wonderful order was not brought about by some great and wise designer, the only other possible explanation is that it happened *by chance*. Innumerable little particles of matter, whirling around in space without any plan or regularity, *just happened* to meet and to combine. Some combined to form the sun, others combined to form the earth, others through long periods of time combined to form men and animals, plants and flowers. Whatever we see, if this explanation is accepted, came about without any guiding intelligence.

Such an explanation is an altogether impossible one. Our common sense refuses to accept it. Consider for a moment an expensive and delicately constructed watch, a watch that keeps perfect time. Could such a watch be *the result of chance?* Does not the fact that it keeps time as it does prove that it was *made for the purpose of keeping time?*

Do the clouds that gather above the earth and send down their refreshing showers *just happen* to exist and to give the earth what it needs? Does it *just happen* that men and animals find all around them the food which they need for the support of life? Does it *just happen* that we have eyes with which to see, ears with which to hear, minds with which to think?

In this book which you are now reading there are many thousands of letters—of *a*'s and *b*'s and *c*'s, and so forth.

Imagine that all of these thousands of letters are painted on little pieces of wood, and that some giant puts them all in a huge barrel and shakes them up, and then empties them on some large flat surface. Is there any chance whatsoever that all these letters will arrange themselves in order so as to form the sentences and paragraphs which you have been reading? We know beyond the possibility of any doubt—and we could prove the point mathematically by the law of chance—that they would never fall in any such order if the giant continued emptying his barrel for millions of years. But these persons who deny the existence of a supreme Designer are asking us to believe something still more incredible. They are asking us to believe that this immense universe, full of so great a number of things most delicately arranged, is the result of blind chance.

Luther Burbank is greatly admired because by experimenting with fruits and vegetables and by crossing one species with another he succeeded in producing new varieties. But Luther Burbank never *made* a living thing; he merely *brought about changes* in living things. Now, if chance really did bring into existence the thousands of living things which we see, why is it that chance, when we give it every possible opportunity to work and even help it, does not produce any living thing today? There are scientists who have spent a great deal of time in the effort to produce a single living cell. A cell is a very simple and tiny thing. We know what its structure is and what materials enter into it. But we cannot make one of these tiny cells, nor do we find that chance is making any cells. To say that a living cell is not

He might by chance write a few words of five or six letters . . . but one complete paragraph would prove his possession of a mind.

the work of some intelligent Designer is just as ridiculous as to say that this book which you are holding in your hands came into existence because particles of paper, cloth, and ink *happened* to meet and to unite in such a way as to result in a book.

CONCLUSION. Whether we look upon the little violet growing in the shady woods, or whether we lift our eyes to the innumerable stars in the heavens, we see everywhere evidence of wonderful design, of wise and loving purpose. When Lord Kelvin, another great scientist, was nearing the end of his long and useful career, he said in a presidential address to the British Association: "Overwhelming proofs of intelligence and benevolent design lie around us . . . teaching us that all living things depend upon one ever-acting Creator and Ruler." The universe proclaims the existence of a Supreme Being, a Being of incredible wisdom, power, and goodness. This Supreme Being we call God.

POINTS FOR REVIEW AND DISCUSSION

1. What does an explorer know if he discovers a ruined dwelling in some part of the world where nobody now lives? How does he know that this dwelling was not the result of chance?

2. Name a number of things which you have seen which certainly indicate design and which were not designed by man.

3. Express your opinion of the following statement: "How are we to explain the manifestations of life on our planet? Millions of years ago nothing existed except great masses of watery particles. Constantly agitated, whirled unceasingly to and fro, some fortunate

ones among these particles chanced to meet in such a way as to form a tiny living thing. From such simple beginnings life gradually developed into the higher forms which we see around about us today."

4. If ten thousand monkeys picked at ten thousand typewriters for an entire day, how many monosyllabic words might they write? How many complete sentences? How many complete and coherent paragraphs? What conclusion do you draw concerning chance as an explanation for the order in the universe? What conclusion would you draw if one of the monkeys *did* write a perfectly correct paragraph?

THE NEXT LESSON

In this lesson we have proved from the design seen in the universe that God exists. But the things thus designed continue to exist and to accomplish their purpose because of certain *laws* which govern their activity. The next lesson will show that these laws are another proof for the existence of God.

Reasoning is too wide!
Design — couldn't happen by chance
∴ a divine Intelligence.
Oh no! ∴ an Intelligence.

THE PROOF FROM PHYSICAL LAW

AWS PROVE THE EX-
ISTENCE OF GOD.
In our last lesson we saw that there was
ample evidence of purpose in the universe. Very many things, of which the
human ear is but one example, are evidently made to do
certain things. From this fact we reasoned to the existence
of a supreme Intelligence.

A second thing which we observe in the universe is the
wonderful regularity with which each part of it acts. In
other words, the universe is governed by certain *laws*. These
laws provide another proof of the existence of God.

EXAMPLES OF LAWS. The movement of the innumerable bodies filling the heavens is governed by laws. Astron-
omers can tell to a second the time of the rising or setting
of a star, or the beginning and ending of an eclipse. Very
shortly after a new comet has appeared its orbit can be
determined. So accurate are the heavenly bodies in their

motion that no human accuracy can rival theirs. At the United States Naval Observatory is one of the most carefully constructed clocks in the world. Despite so many efforts to make this clock perfect and to protect it against vibration and changes in temperature, it is not as accurate as the huge earth in its motion around the sun. The clock loses and gains, but the earth does not.

In biology we learn of the wonderful laws governing life. Plants and animals develop from minute cells in a way which is always uniform. The great Catholic scientist Mendel discovered laws governing the transmission of traits from parent to offspring, so that now we know how many white, red, and pink flowers will appear in each generation if we cross a white flower and a red one. The microscopic particles that govern this process are called *genes;* in some animals and plants they are so small that even the microscope fails to reveal them, yet we know that they have the power to bring about such great results.

In physics we learn about the laws of light, heat, sound, and electricity. Think for a moment of the remarkable laws that control the motion of radio waves. Day after day these laws operate in precisely the same manner, and it is for that reason that we can listen to our favorite program despite the fact that the ether is filled with waves from a dozen stations. The maker of our radio has made it possible for us to catch the set of waves we desire because he knew the laws that govern their motion.

Wonderful, too, are the laws of affinity and attraction in chemistry. Various laws of chemistry appear in our own bodies. Except on the warmest days in summer your body is always much warmer than the air around about it—it is, to be precise, at a temperature just one and two-fifths degrees less than a hundred. Why is this? It is because there is a slow fire burning within you at all times according to the laws of chemistry. Our human furnace is so delicately and accurately adjusted that the heat never becomes greater or less as long as we are in good health.

It would take you many years to master the laws of all the sciences. The man who understood them all would be considered very wise; yet how little would he really understand! We are constantly discovering new laws. Fifty years ago who would have been able to imagine the radio, sound projection, television, the electric eye, and hundreds of other marvels of science? All of these inventions were made possible by the discovery of certain laws. And who can imagine how many more wonderful things will exist fifty years from now? It would certainly be rash to say that we know a tenth of the laws that are operating in the universe today, and it is quite possible that we do not know even so much as a thousandth of them.

HARMONY AMONG LAWS. Still more wonderful than the laws themselves is the harmony that exists among them. Year after year and century after century the universe continues to exist. The seasons come and go in regular order. Men, animals, and plants have all that they need for the support of life. Men and animals consume oxygen and give forth carbon dioxide, and plants breathe in carbon dioxide and give forth oxygen, and thus both have a constant supply of what they need. Both find, too, all the food they need for their nourishment. The sun draws up moisture from oceans, lakes, and streams, and this moisture falls upon the earth again in the form of rain. The forces of nature do not act in such a way as to cause destruction or confusion. They act harmoniously and for the benefit of living things. We live in security because we know what to expect, and we know what to expect because physical laws are constant.

ORIGIN OF PHYSICAL LAWS. Scientists, as we have seen, have told us that these laws exist. But is this answer sufficient? Does it explain everything? Does it answer the questions: Where do laws come from? Why do we have them?

The last question can more easily be answered first. It is quite evident that, if we did not have laws, no one could live. Suppose that no law governed the motion of the heavenly bodies, and that one of them, wandering aimlessly about, should meet the earth at the terrific speed which scientists tell us these bodies have. We can get some idea of the result by thinking of a railroad train traveling at ninety miles an hour and striking an auto. There would be destruction for the auto and death for its occupants. Suppose there were no such law as that of gravitation. If we threw a ball into the air, perhaps it might come down and perhaps it might continue going up. Or suppose that we threw water on a fire, expecting to put it out, and that, instead of extinguishing the fire, the water exploded. Without laws, we could never foresee what was going to happen. We would have nothing but confusion—but we would not have it for any length of time, for without laws all life would soon come to an end.

LAWS EASILY KNOWN. Another thing worthy of note in the laws of nature is the ease with which we can learn what to expect of those laws upon which our lives depend. Many centuries ago Mount Vesuvius suddenly erupted and covered with masses of burning lava the entire city of Pompeii. A few years ago a man and his wife were walking on one of the glaciers of Mount Ranier when the great mass of ice opened without warning beneath their very feet and buried them forever in a frozen grave. Both of these events were the result of the operation of certain physical laws, but men could not easily learn what the laws were, and so could not protect themselves against them. What if all the laws of nature were of this kind? Our lives then would be full of peril and of constant apprehension. But the laws of nature for the most part are not of this kind. They are laws which work in such a way that we can easily learn what to expect. It is true that scientists are struggling almost in vain to discover the laws underlying certain diseases. But these cases are rare, as is proved by the fact that mankind has still survived and that we can all hope to live our lives in peace and comfort if we are willing to exercise due care.

OUR SECOND QUESTION. Our second question was: Where do physical laws come from? This question can be easily answered if we remember that these laws must have come (1) from the physical bodies themselves, (2) from chance, or (3) from some superior Intelligence. Let us consider each of these possibilities.

1. *Physical Laws Are Not Made by Physical Bodies.* Did you ever observe that a pile of snow grows smaller even though the sun is not causing it to melt and even though the temperature is below the freezing point? Why is this? It is because water when in the form of snow is able to evaporate without melting. The result is that the air contains the necessary amount of moisture even in very cold climates. But are we to imagine that *the snow* thought all this out and decided to give itself this property? Such an explanation is of course ridiculous.

The point becomes still clearer if we consider some of the wonderful habits of animals. The hunting wasp (which is the ordinary wasp with which you are familiar) lays its eggs in a clay nest, and in this nest the eggs hatch and become larvae. These larvae must have food. The wasp, therefore, stings a caterpillar, a locust, or some other insect in that one spot where the wasp's sting will not kill it, but will simply put it to sleep as ether puts us to sleep. Then, when the eggs hatch, the larvae find at hand food which is not completely dried up, as would be the case if the wasp had killed the insect instead of anesthetizing it. How did the wasp learn how to do this? Not from its mother, for it never saw its mother. Not from practice, for it does it correctly the first time. It did not *learn* this method of providing food at all; it was *born with* the ability to act in this way. This physical law, one of the many that govern the lives of wasps, was not the creation of the wasp itself.

We see many other remarkable habits in the ant, the bee, the spider, the beaver, and many other animals. Some of these animals do things so perfectly that man cannot duplicate or reproduce them. The beaver, for example, eats away at the trunk of a tall tree until it falls just in that position where the beaver wants it to be for the building of the beaver dam. How did the beaver know that it could make the tree fall at all? A little child hacks away at plants with a knife and is surprised when they fall down. And if you became a lumberjack, you would need a number of lessons before you could fell trees so as to make them fall where they should fall. The beaver, then, acts in this respect more intelligently than man. But we know that this is not due to the fact that the beaver *reasons* about the matter; first, because if beavers reasoned, not all of them would act in precisely the same way, but some would do one thing and some another; secondly, because they fell the trees perfectly from the very beginning; and thirdly, because if the beaver had a mind capable of reasoning out a thing like this, it would be able to act intelligently in many other ways. But the beaver, like all other animals, does a few things in a very intelligent way, and is completely lacking in intelligence in all other respects. It is therefore evident that these laws which cause animals to act consistently in certain ways for the production of certain ends were not made by themselves.

2. *Physical Laws Are Not the Result of Chance.* Shall we say, then, that these laws are the result of chance? Was it by chance that the hunting wasp discovered where to sting

Years and years of effort and experiment enabled man to make an artificial honeycomb not nearly as perfect as that of the bee. . . . From what source did the bee derive its cunning art?

the caterpillar? Our mind refuses to accept any such explanation. It is true that wasps, after stinging many insects, might finally have stung one in that one small spot where the poison of the sting would put the insect to sleep instead of killing it. But why, after once doing this, should wasps continue to sting insects in that one spot? How do they know that it is desirable for the insect to be sleeping rather than dead? Wasps do not see their eggs hatch into larvae, and they do not see them feeding. They know no more about what the larvae need than a child in the Arctic regions who has never seen a wasp or read about one. Does *chance,* then, cause wasps to act uniformly in the one way which makes it possible for their larvae to live? Why should chance so favor the wasps? How much chance could do for us if it does so wonderful a thing for wasps!

3. *Physical Laws Are Made by Some Superior Intelligence.* The only explanation which remains is that all these physical laws are the product of some superior intelligence. This intelligence foresaw what was desirable or necessary and provided for it by giving to physical bodies certain ways of acting which would result in the effects which we see. This intelligence was very great indeed, for it was able, first of all, to make provision for millions and millions of different things; and secondly, it was able to put these ways of acting into living and non-living things. If you find it so difficult to teach a dog some simple trick, how would you proceed in teaching the ant, the bee, the wasp, the spider, and the beaver to do what they do? You could never teach them these things at all; still less could you do what this

supreme Intelligence has done—*give* them the power without teaching it to them.

LAWS PROVE THE EXISTENCE OF GOD. Since these laws exist, and since they are not the product of the physical bodies themselves or of chance, they must be caused by some intelligence which exists independently of the universe. An intelligence capable of doing these things is so perfect, so vastly superior to any other intelligence, so unlimited in its activity, that we are justified in saying that it is infinite. An infinitely intelligent being is called God. Therefore God exists.

POINTS FOR REVIEW AND DISCUSSION

1. Let each member of the class describe some physical law from the sciences or the lives of animals. Consult your textbooks, encyclopedias, or Fabre's works.

2. Express your opinion as to whether these laws are the same now as they were five hundred years ago.

3. Discuss the truth of the following proposition: "The fact that certain additional laws can be made to operate, as happens when men develop a breed of hunting dogs, does not prove that many other laws were not the result of God's action."

4. Prove that some physical laws are very evidently not the result either of the physical bodies in which they are found or of chance.

5. Some object that the laws of nature are so full of imperfections that we cannot ascribe them to an intelligent being. Discuss this objection. Are the imperfections really great and numerous? May even imperfections have a purpose which escapes us? Is it necessary that every work of God should be altogether free from any limitation?

THE NEXT LESSON

We have seen that physical laws prove the existence of God. But there is another kind of law which we find in the world—the moral law which governs the free actions of men. What does this law indicate concerning God? This will be the question taken up in the next lesson.

CHAPTER FOUR

THE PROOF FROM CONSCIENCE

**ORAL LAWS ARE ALSO NECESSARY.** It has already been said that confusion, disorder, and ruin would be the result if there were no laws. But the laws to which we referred were physical laws—laws governing the activity of things which we can see or feel. Man, having a physical body, is subject to these physical laws in the same manner as any physical body. Man is just as much subject to the law of gravitation as is the stone. But in addition to a body man has a soul, and that soul has a power not possessed by any other living thing on earth; it has the power of free and deliberate choice. The animal, which at times seems almost intelligent, is forced to act as it does by instinct, which is nothing more than blind impulses directing the animal in its actions. Proof of this may be seen in the fact that animals, generation after generation, act in the same way and do what their nature leads them to do. Man alone is able freely and deliberately to choose and direct his own actions.

He has a power (the intellect) which shows him what is good and what is bad in an action, and he has another power (the will) which can choose to do or not to do the thing in question. This power of choosing which man possesses can do very great good or very great harm. St. Peter and St. Paul chose to undergo martyrdom for the sake of Christ, and that was good. Cromwell chose to persecute the Church of God, and that was bad. Unless there is a law governing man in his choice of what he is to do, worse confusion would result than if all the physical laws of which we have spoken did not exist.

THE MORAL LAW. But there is a law governing man in his choice of what to do, and this is the moral law. The moral law says that we must do the things that are good, such as to tell the truth, to be just, to be helpful; and that we must avoid the things that are bad, such as to lie, to be dishonest, to be hurtful to others. This law is made known to us by our own intellect, which sees the rightness or the wrongness of the thing we wish to do; and the act of the intellect by which we judge what is morally good or bad is called conscience. Let us see what we can learn from the way man's conscience acts.

CONSCIENCE IS UNIVERSAL. First of all, we find conscience in all men. As soon as we are able to reason, we begin to see that some actions are good and other actions bad. Do we not feel guilty when we break a solemn promise? Are we not ashamed when we tell a deliberate lie? If, driving our auto recklessly and at a high speed while laughing with a carful of boisterous friends, we ran down and killed an innocent child, would we not regret it for the rest of our life? It is true that, if children are not educated as they should be, or if later they become the slaves of bad habits, the interior voice of conscience will not ring out as clearly and strongly as it should. But that voice never has been and *never can be entirely hushed*. It continues to try to make itself heard, and it does make itself heard in some things at least even in the worst of men. This is true today, and it was true in the past. *All races of which we have any record* saw the difference between right and wrong.

CONSCIENCE IS IMPERATIVE. What do we mean when we say that conscience is imperative? We mean that it says to us that we *must* do or avoid certain things. It does not simply say that it would be *advisable* to act in a certain way; it says rather that it is *obligatory* upon us to act in a certain way.

Some newspapers occasionally publish columns called 'Embarrassing Moments,' in which are published stories told by persons who were covered with confusion because of some stupid or thoughtless thing which they had done. You would be embarrassed, for example, if you made some very silly answer in class, or if you spilled your plate in your lap at a party. Some persons suffer very much when they do something of this kind, and are almost afraid to show themselves in public again.

But note this: they may feel terribly *ashamed*, but they do not feel *guilty*. They have made people laugh at them or pity them, but they do not feel that they have committed a moral wrong.

Conscience is something altogether different. The wrong which we have done may have been committed in secret. Nobody else knows about it. What makes us suffer is not that we have done something ignorant or silly, but that we have done something *wrong*. Conscience does not say: "It will be prudent for you to act in such or such a way if you do not wish to make yourself ridiculous." Conscience does not use any language such as that. It says, absolutely, positively, and without leaving room for argument: "You *must* do this; you *are bound* to do that." If, for example, we are tempted to tell a lie about somebody else in order to save ourselves from some difficulty, our conscience immediately warns us that we *must* not do such a thing. This is what we mean when we say that conscience is imperative.

CONSCIENCE POINTS TO A PERSON. Furthermore, our conscience lets us know that by doing what is wrong we will offend some *person*. Even when the deed is utterly secret, this person *knows* that it was done. And if this were not the case, there would be no such thing as conscience at all. Nothing can be morally wrong unless there is a law against it, and there can be no law unless there is a lawgiver. Who is the person who forbade the thing as something wrong? It is not ourselves, for if we chose to say that the thing was wrong, why not now choose to say that it is right, and then our conscience will not bother us any more? It cannot be other men, for if it were the end of the world and we murdered the only other human being still alive, we would feel that it was wrong. This person is not ourselves. This person is not other men. This person is in-

His conscience tormented him . . . "and casting down the pieces of silver in the temple, he departed: and went and hanged himself with an halter" (Matthew 27:5).

visible. This person lets us know what he desires without using words.

CONSCIENCE THREATENS. Again, conscience does not merely warn us that we *must do* a certain thing; it also warns us that there will be a punishment if we refuse to do it. At the moment when we are disobeying our conscience we feel *guilty,* but sooner or later we also feel *afraid.* We know that this lawgiver means what he says. We feel uneasy. We should like to undo what we have done and to get rid of our guilt. We know that, sometime or other, we must face an accounting.

CONSCIENCE AND HAPPINESS. Those who follow the dictates of their conscience enjoy the greatest possible peace. But those who disobey the voice of conscience are tormented in mind. Judas in despair went out and hanged himself with a halter. Every year fugitives from justice voluntarily surrender to the police because they can no longer endure the reproaches of their conscience. How many pathetic stories there are of persons driven mad by the memory of their evil deeds! Why has conscience this strange power to torment us, even when no man knows or cares what we have done?

CONSCIENCE PROVES THE EXISTENCE OF GOD. There is only one possible explanation for the appearance of conscience among all men of all times and for the manner in which it manifests itself. Conscience, that voice which tells us what is morally right or wrong, cannot result from the fact that we have made laws for ourselves, nor from the fact that society has said that certain things are morally right or wrong. It can be explained only by the fact that there is some supreme lawgiver in whose eyes there is a difference between good and evil and who gave man an intellect capable of seeing this difference. This lawgiver must be most wise and good, for wisdom and goodness appear everywhere in his moral law. He must be most powerful, for he can make known his wishes to all men through conscience without the use of any words. This lawgiver can be none other than God.

POINTS FOR REVIEW AND DISCUSSION

1. Name the five things worthy of notice in conscience which are explained in this chapter.

2. To cause a man's death by making a false charge against him was wrong from the beginning of the world, is wrong now, and always will be wrong. Answer the following questions:

a. Would such an action be wrong if it had not been *forbidden?*

b. If there are civil laws against it, was it wrong before those laws were made?

c. Would it be wrong even in the midst of a savage tribe which did not consider it wrong?

d. Who must have made it wrong if it was not the state or society?

3. We have used conscience as a proof for the existence of God. But a difficulty arises from the fact that some men do not seem to have a conscience. For example, there have been tribes which killed unwanted or physically defective children. Some of the following statements throw light on this difficulty, and others have no bearing on it. Discuss the statements:

a. Tribes which kill defective children have lost the power to reason.

b. Even the worst nations have correct consciences concerning some points of the moral law.

c. It is probably true that those who kill infants in this way realize at some time during their lives, perhaps vaguely, that the action is wrong.

d. A correct conscience is a gift of the Holy Ghost, and therefore we cannot expect to find conscience in savage tribes of non-Catholics.

e. Custom and bad education can create false consciences. Our proof does not depend upon the existence of correct consciences in all men, but on the very existence of even a partially correct conscience.

THE NEXT LESSON

We have now given three proofs for the existence of God:
1. From design,
2. From physical laws,
3. From the moral law.

An additional argument is found in the fact that belief in God has been found among all men at all times. This is called the argument from history. It will be taken up in the next lesson.

CHAPTER FIVE

THE PROOF FROM HISTORY

OLDEST RACES BELIEVED IN GOD. Men of every race and of every century of which there is any historical record believed in the existence of God. Is this a convincing proof that God exists? No, this belief taken in itself is not a convincing proof; but if we consider all the circumstances connected with this universal conviction, the proof is undoubtedly very strong, and in the minds of some might even be conclusive.

Besides, it is well worth while to know more about this conviction among early races, for the enemies of religion have built up theories which, if not shown to be untrue, would do great harm. These enemies of religion represent the earliest men of whom we have any record as extremely ignorant and superstitious. Primitive man, they say, was afraid of wild animals and of the forces of nature, and so he tried to find comfort and strength in the thought that there was some invisible power to which he could turn for assistance. This invisible power was in the beginning very unlike God as we now conceive Him; the idea of God which we have today (so they declare) is not natural to man, but is a gradual development of old superstitious beliefs under the influence of civilization.

This theory is not true. Father W. Schmidt, who is recognized throughout the world as an authority on the religious beliefs of the very earliest men of whom any record exists, has shown in his book on *The Origin and Growth of Religion* that the earliest peoples believed in one Supreme Being. Their beliefs may be summed up as follows:

1. The Supreme Being is *always* represented as existing forever.
2. The Supreme Being is *often* said to know all things.
3. The Supreme Being is *quite commonly* represented as altogether loving and kind.
4. The Supreme Being is *always* looked upon as unalterably righteous.
5. The Supreme Being is *always* said to possess enormous power, which is often said to be boundless.
6. The Supreme Being is *usually* said to have creative power; and although we lack evidence as to what some of the primitive races thought on this point, there is no case where creative power is *denied.*
7. The Supreme Being rewards good and punishes evil; and in the *great* majority of cases this reward or punishment occurs in the next world.

LATER BELIEF IN GOD. The Greeks, the Romans, the Persians, the Chinese, the Babylonians, the Assyrians, and every other nation that has ever existed believed in God. It is true that many of them worshipped more than one God, but among these many gods there was usually one who was superior to the others. The word 'God' occurs in every language used by man.

NATURE OF THIS BELIEF.

The following points in regard to this belief in God deserve to be noted:

First, it is universal in time and place. It is found in every age and in every part of the world.

Secondly, it is common to every type of man, not only to the uneducated, but to the learned; not only to women and children, but to men.

Thirdly, this belief has been tested in every possible way. It has been proved by solid arguments to be true. Every possible objection against it has been answered. On the other hand, thousands of persons throughout the centuries have attempted to attack the idea, but no one of them has ever produced a sensible and solid argument in support of his position.

Fourthly, this belief has constantly been held by men despite the fact that they would be more free to do as they wished if they did not hold it. They hold it because they are convinced of its truth.

Fifthly, this belief has to do with a matter of vital concern to man. It makes a great difference to him, both in this life and in the next, whether God exists or does not exist. Can we believe that man's reason fails him in a matter such as this?

Sixthly, those who believe in God and live according to their belief are contented, happy, and useful; but to deny that God exists has never added to the real happiness of the human race or made anyone morally better.

From the first dawn of history down to the present day belief in God has been universal, not in the sense that every man without exception has believed in God, but in the sense that the belief has been extremely widespread at every period of time. The skin-clad hunter of centuries ago knelt and raised his eyes and his heart to heaven, where he believed an all-powerful Father dwelt. The greatest minds of the present day have the same belief. Scientists, poets, historians—scholarly men of every kind—kneel in reverence before the Supreme Being.

AN OBJECTION ANSWERED. It may be objected that for centuries men believed that the sun moved around the earth, and that this belief was nevertheless not true. But in the first place it is not certain that *all* men believed this. In the second place this belief was for a long time not tested, checked, and verified. All that men could say was that the sun *looked as if* it moved around the earth. But when there is question of moving bodies, the eye alone is not always a sufficient guide; we must oftentimes touch and feel the body which we think is moving, or use other means to determine whether or not it is moving. In the course of time men *did* test their belief that the sun moved around the earth, and found that they were wrong. Even here reason did not fail man as soon as man made a serious effort to use his reason. Why did man not make this effort sooner? Partly because it did not make any great practical difference whether the sun moved around the earth or the earth around the sun; partly because this question could not be settled until mathematics had been developed to a high point of perfection.

A million church spires pointing heavenward today . . . and the old records of earliest man . . . prove alike that the human mind unchangeably accepts the existence of a God.

If we had asked men who believed that the sun moved around the earth: "Have you checked up on this matter? Are you *certain* of this, or does it merely *look that way* to you?" they would have been forced to answer that it merely looked that way. And as a matter of fact, not very many centuries had passed before thoughtful men *did* check up on the matter, finding the old impression incorrect.

But if we ask men who believe in the existence of God: "Have you ever attempted to verify your belief?" the answer would be:

"This belief has been verified in every way known to the human mind. It is not a belief where the eyes can expose us to error, as in the old case of men's belief in the movement of the sun, but it is a belief which depends upon the intellect more than it does on the senses. If our belief in God is not true, we ought logically to refuse to believe any conclusion ever reached by our intellect. If the entire human race is in error on this matter, we are living in a nightmare; we are never reasoning, but only imagining that we reason. Our intellect has failed us at the most vital point, and it is useless longer to attempt to arrive at truth concerning those things that most closely concern us."

GREAT MEN BELIEVE IN GOD. The greatest minds of all ages have believed in God. Not only the saints of the Church, but statesmen, poets, scientists, and artists have given testimony to their conviction that a Supreme Being exists. Kneller, in *Christianity and the Leaders of Modern Science,* mentions over one hundred and sixty eminent scientists of the nineteenth century who believed firmly in God. Almost all the signers of our own Declaration of Independence were sincere believers. George Washington placed his trust in God, and was frequently on his knees at times of special peril. When the Constitutional Convention, which met in Philadelphia to draft the constitution of the new nation, was experiencing difficulty in reaching an agreement, Benjamin Franklin urged the members to have recourse to prayer, and proposed the following motion:

That henceforth prayers, imploring the assistance of Heaven and its blessing on our deliberations, be held in this assembly every morning before we proceed to business; and that one or more of the clergy of this city be requested to officiate at that service.

When we say, then, that the universal conviction of mankind is an argument for the existence of God, we do not mean to imply that whatever all men believe to be true must be true. This belief is different from other beliefs. It has been so thoroughly investigated, and pertains to a matter of such importance, that it is impossible for us to think that the human intellect has been in error. If the intellects of so many great, good, and learned men have been deceived, the intellects of the little handful of men who say that God does not exist could still more easily be deceived, and the consequence would be that all men, great and small alike, are incapable of discovering the truth in a matter of such importance.

It is impossible for us to accept a theory such as this. Man's intellect, which constantly gives such proofs of brilliancy and power, is certainly able to determine whether or not a First Cause exists. The conclusions of any one man might possibly be wrong, but the conclusion reached by the best intellects of every age and race cannot be wrong. The universal conviction of mankind is a proof of the existence of God.

POINTS FOR REVIEW AND DISCUSSION

1. What does the most recent research of Father W. Schmidt tell us concerning the belief in God of the very earliest races?

2. Mention some characteristics of the universal belief in God.

3. The following are propositions now held, or at one time held, by all men or by very many men. In connection with which is universal consent a proof of the truth of the proposition? In which is it not a proof? What is the reason for the difference?
   a. Fire burns.
   b. Clouds are composed of white material.
   c. The sun moves around the earth.
   d. The moon is larger than Mars.
   e. Water freezes.
   f. God exists.

4. Some nations have believed in many gods. Why does this fact not weaken the argument given in this chapter?

THE NEXT LESSON

We have now studied four proofs for the existence of God. One argument remains which is the most absolutely unanswerable of all. But it is more subtle and difficult than the ones already given. It would not be a disgrace if your class found it hard, for it is a keen argument. We have tried to explain it so that it can be easily understood. It is found in the next two lessons, and you and your teacher can decide whether to take these lessons or to omit them.

THE PRINCIPLE OF CAUSALITY

VERY EFFECT REQUIRES A CAUSE. The paper at which you are now looking is white. Let us suppose that it suddenly turns into a brilliant crimson. What would you think? What would be your spontaneous and necessary reaction? You would ask yourself at once: "What made it turn crimson?" Possibly there was some chemical in the paper which, when affected by the light for a certain length of time, made the paper change its color. Possibly something has happened to the sun or to the atmosphere. Possibly someone has jokingly slipped a piece of crimson glass between your eyes and the paper. Possibly your eyes themselves have been affected by some disease. All these things may occur to you as possibilities. But one thing simply could not occur to you as a possibility: you would never think that the paper changed from white to crimson without any reason. When things happen, there is something there to make them happen. If a window that was closed becomes open, something or some-

one opened it. If an airplane sails gracefully through the air, there is some source of power that makes it move. If your fish line gives a sudden jerk, there is something at the end of it that made it jerk. Things do not just happen. There is always something, either within them or outside them, that causes them to happen.

KINDS OF CAUSES. There are many kinds of causes, which are taken up in detail in courses on philosophy. To learn about them now would not be difficult, but it is not necessary that we should do so. Only one cause is of interest to us here, and that is the *efficient cause*. But it will be worth while to see quickly what some other causes are by means of a simple example.

Let us suppose that Mary and Agnes are sisters, and that Mary asks Agnes to bake a cake like one which they enjoyed some time before at a friend's house. Agnes does what Mary wishes, and finally the cake is made and ready to eat. What are the causes that resulted in the cake? These causes are as follows:

1. Mary's appeal to Agnes, and the influence she exerted on her to get her to make the cake. (The *moral efficient* cause.)
2. Agnes' desire to please Mary. (The *final* cause.)
3. The materials used by Agnes—the flour, eggs, sugar, and so forth. (The *material* cause.)
4. The instruments and machines used by Agnes—the stove, the spoons, the egg-beater, and so forth. (The *instrumental* cause.)
5. The cake which Mary had proposed to Agnes as a model. (The *exemplary* cause.)
6. Agnes herself, who actually made the cake. She was the *efficient* cause.

This is very simple. You yourself can see and tell how these six kinds of causes are found in such cases as the following: (a) If you are a member of a football team which plays on a vacant lot, and the other members of the team persuade you to erect goal posts. (b) If your teacher suggests that you construct a grotto for a statue of the Blessed Virgin. (c) If the members of your camping party persuade you to build a wharf at which to tie your canoe.

We must not forget that not all six causes are found in every kind of action. Sometimes nobody urges or persuades us to do what we do. Sometimes we do not need any materials. Sometimes we do not need any instruments or tools. But there is one cause that must always be present whenever an effect is produced, and that is the *efficient* cause. The efficient cause is the person or thing that *actually makes the effect exist.* The efficient cause answers the question: "Who or what did it?"

THE PRINCIPLE OF CAUSALITY. Knowing, as we have always known, that whatever begins to exist must have a cause, we can easily tell what the *principle of causality* is. The principle of causality is stated as follows: Whatever begins to exist must have a reason for its existence outside of itself.

PROOF OF THE PRINCIPLE. If a thing begins to exist, it did not exist at all before it began to exist. Something had to make it begin to exist. That fact is so evident that it is useless to prove it. Look for a moment at the blackboard in the classroom and imagine that a chalk mark suddenly appears on it. Did somebody or something make the

*A track . . . a broken twig . . . a bent tuft of grass . . .
these tell the pathfinder that man or beast has passed by
. . . for from the effect we can reason to the nature of the
cause.*

chalk mark? Of course; there is no argument about that. The chalk mark began to exist, and therefore it must have a reason for its existence. But the reason for the existence of the chalk mark cannot be the chalk mark itself—it must be something outside or independent of the chalk mark. For if a thing does not exist at all, how can it do anything or produce any effect?

Next year the United States Government will issue a number of new postage stamps and new one-dollar bills. Must they have a cause for their existence outside themselves?

Ten years from now there may be a thirty-story building where this school now stands. Must that building have a reason for its existence outside itself?

Yesterday thousands of loaves of bread were made by bakers and delivered to customers. Did they have to have a reason for their existence outside themselves?

These examples, and numerous others which we might think of, show us how true and universal the principle of causality is. "Whatever begins to exist must have a reason for its existence outside itself." In other words, it must have an efficient cause.

WHAT THE EFFECT SHOWS. This is all we need to know about the principle of causality. But while we are speaking of causes, we may as well learn one other thing which will be useful later. It is that we can know something about the nature of the cause by studying the nature of the effect.

Just as we know that gasoline *must have something in it* which enables it to give motion to an automobile, so whenever we see an effect we know something about the cause which produced the effect.

A rich rose gives us the sensation of fragrance. But pennies, nickles, and quarters do not produce any such sensation. Therefore there is something in the rose which is not in coins and which is of such a nature that it can produce this sensation.

Song birds give us pleasure by their singing. But if you pick up a stone and hold it to your ear, you will never hear anything. Therefore the birds have a power which the stone does not possess.

You yourselves have learned something about causes. You have grasped new ideas and have answered questions intelligently. This would not have happened if there had been sacks of flour in the desks where you are sitting. Therefore you have a power which sacks of flour do not have.

But although we can always learn *something* about the nature of the cause by examining the effect, it does not follow that we can learn *everything* about it. We have learned enough about the cause of typhoid fever to be able to control it. Almost nobody would die of typhoid if he took the necessary precautions. But there are other diseases concerning which we do not know as much, and so people frequently die of them. But at least we know this much, that the cause is something which invades the human organism. In our effort to control these diseases we do not waste time looking for other kinds of causes. And so in general we are certain of this:

The effect reveals something concerning the nature of the cause.

THE PRINCIPLE OF CAUSALITY

SUMMARY. There are many kinds of causes, and a knowledge of them helps us to think clearly and correctly. But our chief interest in this book is in the *efficient* cause, which is that cause which actually brings the effect into existence. Whenever a thing does not exist at one time and is later found to exist, there must have been an efficient cause of its existence. The nature of the effect tells us something about the nature of the cause, but this knowledge, while correct as far as it goes, is often incomplete.

POINTS FOR REVIEW AND DISCUSSION

1. Is it necessary to know precisely what the cause is in order to be certain that some cause must exist? Give a reason for your answer.

2. The philosopher Hume did not believe in efficient causes. Tell of something which you saw today which proves that Hume was wrong.

3. In the following list of effects, in which cases could you find the cause by sight or perception, and in which cases would you be certain of the cause only by reasoning about it? (1) The ticking sound coming from your watch. (2) A blister on your foot which results from shoes that are too large. (3) The music of a band in a parade. (4) A lightning flash. (5) The peace that comes after a good confession. (6) The drought of 1934. (7) The return to its loft of a homing pigeon.

4. Show how a doctor uses the principle of causality in making a diagnosis; how an auto mechanic uses it in repairing your machine; how a detective uses it in tracking down clues.

5. Imagine that you are lying on the grass with your dog at your side, and that the dog looks at you and says: "I wish to be baptized

in the Catholic Church." What would the principle of causality tell us about what must have happened to the dog, assuming that you are able to verify the fact that there was no deception or trick in the matter and that the dog actually said and meant these words?

THE NEXT LESSON

In the next lesson we will take what we have learned about efficient causes and prove that God must exist. This proof is the strongest of all that we have. Nobody can refute it. All anyone can do is to refuse to discuss it, which shows that he is either unable or unwilling to think about this matter.

CHAPTER SEVEN

THE PROOF FROM CAUSALITY

ECESSITY OF AN UN-CAUSED CAUSE. We saw in the last lesson that, whenever a thing begins to exist when it did not exist before, there must be some efficient cause which makes it begin to exist. Imagine that you are holding your hand, palm up, in front of you, and that suddenly a silver dollar appears on your palm. You *know* with a certainty which excludes all doubt that somebody must have made that silver dollar and that somebody or something must have made it appear on your palm. This is a thing which is so clear and undeniable that no one can doubt or deny it. It is impossible for anything to begin to exist without an efficient cause.

But now let us think for a moment of these things which *begin to exist*. If there were nothing at all in the universe except things which of their nature *must begin to exist,* would the universe itself exist? Would there be any world at all if every single thing in the world was a thing which at one time was a mere possibility and which at some later time became an actuality?

THE PRINCIPLE ILLUSTRATED. Let us take some one thing existing today as an example, for what we learn about this one thing will be true of any other thing. Let us take the dog that you see running about when you go home after school in the afternoon.

This dog had a father and a mother—his efficient causes —and they had fathers and mothers, and so on back for many generations.

Some people will say that, when we get back far enough, we will find that we do not have dogs any more, but some other animal, such as a rat, from which dogs developed. The evidence for this does not seem to be conclusive, but let us imagine for the sake of argument that dogs did develop from some other kind of animal. These animals had fathers and mothers too, and so we keep on going back for many more generations.

The same persons who say that the dog developed from the rat will say that the rat developed from some simple little living thing with only one cell in it, and that this living thing with one cell developed from something which was not alive at all. Very well; let them have their way for the sake of argument. Then the complete life history of the dog will take us back through a very long series of efficient causes to things which bear very little resemblance to the dog which we see, but which nevertheless had something to do with its existence.

Now take the very first of this long series. It could not

have existed of itself; for if a dog cannot exist of itself, still less could the inferior thing from which the dog developed. Therefore it must have been made by something else. Did this 'something else' depend on some other thing for its existence? We cannot go on forever with a chain of effects like this. Sooner or later we must get back to some cause *which does not depend on another cause*. No matter how long the chain is, the first link in it cannot be an effect, for we have already seen that every effect must have a cause which precedes it.

A FURTHER EXAMPLE. Let us take another example. If you look around this classroom, you will undoubtedly see something that is made of iron—the inkwell in your desk, the metal frame of the desk, the radiator, or the hinges of the door.

This iron was made from ore mined from the earth.

Was the ore always—from the very first instant of its existence—in the same state it was in when mined? Probably not. Long ago it was probably in a molten state, like the hot lava that flows from Mount Vesuvius. Before that it was probably part of a great mass of fiery gaseous substance. In its long history it undoubtedly underwent many changes.

Now, whenever one of these changes took place, there was some cause which made it take place. We have already seen that things do not happen without a cause.

Suppose, then, that we draw on the blackboard a number of dots, each of which is to represent one of the causes that brought the iron ore to its final state when it was mined from the earth. These dots are to give us the complete *history* of the iron ore. They are going to include *every single thing* that had anything to do with making the iron ore be what it is. And we will observe the following rules in making these dots:

1. If a cause is the *effect* of something else, use yellow chalk.
2. If a cause is *not the effect* of anything else, use red chalk.

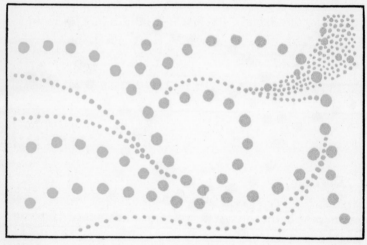

Now you have finished drawing all the dots, and these dots represent every single thing that had anything to do with the existence of the iron ore as we see it today.

Are all the dots drawn with yellow chalk? If they are, we immediately say:

"You have not told the whole story. All your dots, even the very first one, are in yellow. Perhaps you do not know which of the dots represents the very first of the causes, but the first one must be *somewhere*. Wherever it is, it is yellow, for all of them are yellow. That means that the very first of your causes was the effect of something else. Why did you not show the cause of which it is the effect?"

"Pardon me," you answer; "I forgot to put down the cause of the first of my causes." And so you go to the blackboard and make another *yellow* dot.

Are you going to keep this up forever? And even if you

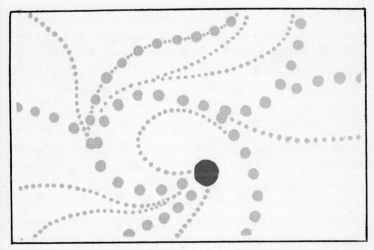

did keep it up forever, even if you could finally make an *infinite number* of yellow dots, you would have failed to explain their existence. The earliest of your causes is always yellow—that is, it is the effect of something else—and you have never told us what that something else is.

But now see what happens if you will finally consent to make just one dot in red. The dot in red is a cause which is not the effect of anything else. It does not need anything outside itself to explain it. It is an uncaused cause. It exists in virtue of its own nature. It is what we call the First Cause.

As soon as you make this one red dot, the story is complete. Everything is explained. One single red dot, one First Cause, solves our difficulty.

THE FIRST CAUSE IS ETERNAL. If the First Cause does not depend upon anything else for its existence, if it exists simply in virtue of its own nature, then it must have existed forever. For imagine, if you will, a time when even the First Cause did not exist. In the first place, you can not imagine any such thing, for if the First Cause is able to exist independently of any action or assistance on the part of anything else, why should it have to wait for any certain moment to begin existing? In the second place, if there ever was a time when the First Cause did not exist, how did it ever begin to exist? You cannot say its nature made it exist, for under your supposition *there was no such nature*. Therefore the First Cause never had a beginning.

Moreover, if the First Cause exists in virtue of its own nature, it will never cease to exist, for it always has its nature, in addition to which it needs nothing at all to make it exist. Therefore the First Cause will never cease to be; and since it has neither beginning nor end, it is eternal.

THE FIRST CAUSE IS INFINITE. All the other things in the universe—all the living beings, all the trees, all the flowers, all the oceans, lakes, and streams, all the precious minerals hidden away in the earth—are things *that had to begin to exist*. There was a time when they did not exist. There was a time when the First Cause existed all alone.

When the First Cause, therefore, began to make other things exist, the First Cause did not construct these things out of material already existing. The First Cause may later have made some things out of material already existing, but certainly the first things made were not made in this way. They were made out of nothing. They began to exist simply because the First Cause willed that they should exist. All that the First Cause had to do was to will that they should exist. But if the First Cause could make one thing out of nothing, it could make any other thing out of nothing. If it made one sun, it could make a million suns. If it made the moon, it could make the earth; and if it made the earth, it could make other earths more beautiful than the first earth. *not conclusive!* It could, in short, make anything it wished to make. What word must we use to describe power such as that? There is only one word that will describe it—Infinite.

Possibly you had to do a little hard thinking in this lesson, but now you understand what Herbert Spencer meant when he said:

"It is absolutely certain that we are in the presence of an infinite, eternal energy, from which all things proceed."

This infinite, eternal energy is known as God.

God, then, is the First Cause, a being uncreated, the cause of all other causes, eternal, infinite, and existing separately from the world.

Just as the giant searchlight pierces the heavens at night and leads the eye to whatever object is illuminated by its finger of light, so this thought leads us always back to God. Whatever we may see—birds, flowers, streams, books, pictures, men and women walking through the streets—must have had a First Cause, must depend on God. What a blessing to be unchangeably convinced of this truth, when so many men are dying by their own hands in despair because they do not believe there is another world in which there is an infinite and eternal God!

POINTS FOR REVIEW AND DISCUSSION

1. Prove that there must be a First Cause which exists of its own nature.

2. Prove that the First Cause is eternal.

3. Prove that the First Cause is infinite.

4. Criticize this statement, found in a textbook on zoölogy now used in some state universities: "Science rejects the theory that life arose by some creative act. Life was produced accidentally when conditions became suitable."

THE NEXT LESSON

We have now completed our proofs from reason for the existence of God. In the next lesson we will try to show what is to be thought of atheism, which denies God's existence.

ATHEISM

OLD MEANING OF ATHEISM. While in these modern times atheism means the denial of God's existence, yet this was not always the meaning of the term. When the term 'atheist' was first coined it was not applied to those who denied the existence of a deity, but referred to men who did not agree with what others thought of God. For example, if you had lived in ancient Greece and did not accept the old gods of the Greeks, you would have been called an atheist even though you believed in God. The early Christians were called atheists, not because they did not believe in God, but because they refused to accept the Roman interpretation of what the Supreme Being was. A real out-and-out denial of the existence of a deity was not popular in those days, but a denial of a current interpretation was frequent. In these modern times atheism has little to do with interpretation; it is rather a complete denial of God's existence, and is becoming more widespread and aggressive than it was in any earlier age. Our 'Age of Reason,' whatever it may have achieved in other respects, deserves rather to be called the 'Age of Bad Reason' because of its easy acceptance of atheistic ideas.

POSITIVE ATHEISTS. Those who openly deny that there is a God are called *positive* atheists. They may be divided into three classes, which differ among themselves in the extent of their hostility to the idea of God.

The first class includes those who affirm that God does not exist and who seek to support their position by some sort of argument. Few if any philosophers who have exerted any influence upon the world belong to this class, and more than one philosopher and man of science, when accused of being atheistic, has indignantly declared that he was misunderstood and misinterpreted. But there have been popular orators of the type of Robert Ingersoll who have attracted crowds of the curious by ridiculing church-going people and by challenging God to strike them dead in thirty seconds if He does indeed exist.

Probably the greatest number of positive atheists are to be found among the extreme materialistic communists of the day. Some of the attacks upon God found in the writings of communist leaders in Soviet Russia are amazing in their violence and hatred.

In the second class of positive atheists are found those scientists who attribute to the matter of the universe some strange and unexplained power of bringing itself into existence, and thus by implication make God unnecessary if not impossible. Although we occasionally find a scientist who positively affirms that God does not exist, the more common attitude is rather a negative one, God's existence being merely ignored. We should not, however, entertain the idea that scientists as a class are atheistic, for many—probably the vast majority—are men of strong religious convictions.

In the third class of positive atheists we may place those who are known as *pantheists*. They affirm that everything is God, and that all the things you see around about you are part of God. To say this is equivalently to deny the existence of a spiritual and infinite Being outside and superior to the material universe, for if the material things of the world are God, God Himself must be material.

PRACTICAL ATHEISTS. Far more numerous than the positive atheists are what we call *practical* atheists. A practical atheist is one who does not defend any theory on the subject of God's existence, but who in practice lives as if God did not exist. There are many thousands of men and women of this type. They do not solve any problem by asking themselves what God thinks and desires. They do not believe in revelation. They do not accept a natural law which emanates from God and which is capable of being known by the light of reason. Creation, redemption, grace and the supernatural life, heaven—all these are ideas that mean nothing to them.

EFFECTS OF PRACTICAL ATHEISM. If God's truth and justice were always foremost in men's minds, we would never have had the World War, we would never have had the Treaty of Versailles with all its bitter consequences, and we would never have had a depression which reduced millions to stark poverty and even to starvation in the midst of an abundance so great that nations destroyed crops and herds in the vain effort to bring back prosperity.

Many prominent leaders of thought and action today are practical atheists. This is true of diplomats and business men, of economists, sociologists, and jurists. Oftentimes they have great zeal for the common welfare, but the means upon which they depend for its promotion are worldly and purely natural.

Years ago men thought that science would bring peace and contentment to the world. Let us pay due tribute to science for its gifts and to scientists for their unselfish labor. But science can never tell us *what we ought to do*. Science can invent some poisonous gas which if dropped from the sky will wipe out every inhabitant. But science is mute when we ask whether it is right to use that gas. Science can tell us how much a man needs for food, clothing, shelter, and recreation in order to live a reasonably normal life, but science, without appealing to the will and the law of God, cannot say whether it is right or wrong for an employer to keep vast profits for himself while giving his employees a pittance insufficient to support life.

Now we are turning to the social sciences for answers to vexing questions. Again let us pay tribute to the social sciences for whatever good they have accomplished. But if the social sciences depend upon human reason alone, if they seek answers to problems without considering the eternal truth of God, they too will fail to bring true peace to the world.

When we consider the modern trend toward practical atheism, it is not surprising to find so many nations today in the throes of political, economic, and religious wars which threaten the very existence of civilization. There is only one remedy: a return to that divine law which enjoins justice and brotherly love upon all men.

WHY MEN ARE ATHEISTS. In every civilized country atheists are to be found, and in many countries there are active societies for the promotion of atheism. We find such societies even on the campuses of some of our own universities. In the city of New York, only a few years ago, twelve thousand children were attending every week Sunday schools whose one purpose was to teach positive atheism. We all know what efforts have been made in Soviet Russia to inspire hatred and contempt for God. How can we explain this widespread belief in a theory so lacking in any reasonable foundation? We must be careful not to judge any man, but the following are at least possible answers to the question:

1. The atheist is different. He believes and preaches things that startle others. Atheism, then, can appeal to man's vanity.

2. To be superior and independent is attractive to us. The atheist makes himself independent even of God.

3. When men have sinned, and when they find it very difficult to observe God's law, they would like if possible to believe that there is no God to whom they are responsible.

4. Young people may sincerely believe in God and yet be unable to give a reason for their belief or to answer the objections of others. If they attend certain universities and sit in

the classrooms of atheistic professors, they are dazzled by the display of brilliant scholarship and are affected by the confident declaration that the Bible is a collection of myths and legends. Thus the foundations of their faith are weakened because they expose themselves to danger before they are prepared to meet it.

5. Protestantism is responsible for much of the atheism that exists. The clergymen of most Protestant sects (the Lutherans are a conspicuous exception to the rule) do not as a body believe in any system of religious truth that is complete, certain, and unchanging. Liberal Protestantism, with its theory of individual interpretation, cannot hold that anything is so certain and so true that it must be believed by all. Young people, then, confused by so many different opinions and unable to discern anywhere a clear and authoritative voice, may easily reach the conclusion that no teaching of religion can be accepted as certain. A perfect example of this process is found in John L. Stoddard, the famous lecturer who in his old age embraced the Catholic faith. In his youth he began to study for the Congregationalist ministry, but found nothing in that church which was able to satisfy his mind. What happened? He says in *Rebuilding a Lost Faith*, page 14:

I, like most Protestants . . . took it for granted that all the calumnies which I had read of 'Rome' were true, and therefore I concluded that conditions which I had found unbearable in Protestantism would be much worse in Catholicism.

Accordingly, although it was a matter on which my soul's eternal welfare might depend, so great were both my ignorance and arrogance, that I made no attempt to investigate the claims and doctrines of the Catholic Church, but chose deliberately Rationalism, whose ardent advocate I then remained for forty years.

6. Finally, we must if we are honest admit that atheism is often an act of rebellion against a religion which has been made to appear unpleasant, narrow, and inconsistent. A few years ago many hundreds of atheists were asked why they were so, and many declared that they had embraced atheism because the religion of their parents had been so unattractive. It is our duty to let our light shine before men. We should always live so that no one can ever say: "What is the use of trying to find God? These people had a good chance to find Him, and they think that they did find Him; but see how they live!" It is unreasonable to speak in this way, for the fact that other persons are poor servants of God does not in any way excuse us from trying to be good ones. Nevertheless, when the mind is clouded and the passions aroused, bad example may easily lead one to lose his faith in God.

ARGUMENTS AGAINST ATHEISM. The arguments against atheism are those explained earlier in this book: the proofs for God's existence drawn from design, physical laws, conscience, history, and the principle of causality. The atheist on his part has no positive arguments to offer. What he calls arguments are only difficulties or objections. His most frequent appeal is to the evil existing in the world. Perhaps genuinely distressed by the pain, the poverty, and the injustice which are found everywhere, he asks how the God whom we depict as so kind and loving can permit such things to occur. He does not realize that without suffering there would be no occasion for patience; without inequalities, no place for mercy and generosity; without peril, no opportunity for fortitude and heroism. He knows nothing of the nature and effects of original sin, and he does not understand that life is a period of trial during which man is free to choose either the evil or the good. Never having thought clearly and fully about God's infinite nature, he assumes that there is no good reason for God's way of acting merely because he with his finite intellect cannot see the reason.

He calls attention to the failure of the Church to correct evils which Scripture itself says cry to heaven for vengeance, and to the sinful lives of some of those who profess allegiance to the Church. But he fails to understand that the Church can only urge men to be good, not force them; nor does his prejudice permit him to see that the thousands of thoroughly good men and women who derive all their ideals and all their strength from the Church are a far better argument for the existence of God than unfaithful Christians are for atheism.

COMPLETE ATHEISM IMPOSSIBLE. But is the atheist so convinced of the truth of his theory that he never has a doubt? We believe that doubts must arise in the atheist's heart, and that he can remain what he is only by closing his eyes to the light and his ears to the voice of truth. St. Paul says:

For the invisible things of Him, from the creation of the world, are clearly seen, being understood from the things that are made; His eternal power also, and divinity. So that they are inexcusable because that, when they knew God, they have not glorified Him as God, or given thanks; but became vain in their thoughts, and their foolish heart was darkened. For professing themselves to be wise, they became fools (Romans 1:20-22).

We who brand the atheist as illogical because the imperfections of the world make him deny God's existence, must resolve now never to permit any scandal to shake our own faith. God remains, and our personal obligations to Him remain, no matter how shamefully any member of the Church may fall.

POINTS FOR REVIEW AND DISCUSSION

1. What was the meaning of 'atheist' in olden times? What is the meaning today?

2. What is a practical atheist? A positive atheist?

3. Why is atheism contrary to reason?

4. Prove that atheism destroys all true moral obligation; that it must lead to a denial of any duty in conscience to act in one way rather than in another.

5. Compare the atheist and the man who believes in God in regard to:
   a. Their reasons for loving their fellow men.
   b. Their reasons for controlling their passions.
   c. Their courage in times of trial.

6. What should be one's attitude toward the societies of atheists found in our country today, even in colleges and universities?

7. Prove the truth of the statement of a popular lecturer (Father Hubbard): "The positive atheist is a practical liar."

8. Are those people who today set up false gods to be considered atheists or polytheists? (The Nazis reviving the worship of Teutonic deities; Lenin-worship in Russia; state-worship in Japan.)

9. A practical atheist acts in all things as if there were no God. Under what condition can a Catholic resemble a practical atheist?

THE NEXT LESSON

Another evil still more prevalent than atheism is agnosticism. If in the course of your life you meet ten thousand different persons, probably one thousand or more of them will be agnostics. In the next lesson we will explain what agnosticism is and why it is wrong.

CHAPTER NINE

AGNOSTICISM

 **IMPORTANCE OF USING OUR REASON WELL.** Reason, when used properly, is a most wonderful gift of God. It was intended to lead us to the knowledge of truth, and in truth is found peace and happiness. On the contrary, the bad use of reason may have terrible effects upon man and his happiness. When reason is not properly used it brings us into error, and in error there can be found nothing but disaster.

Have you ever observed that men reason far more poorly in some fields than they do in others? A druggist who sold poison for medicine would not deceive the people for any length of time, but philosophical quacks can sell the public ideas which are poison for the mind and soul.

We have said that the 'Age of Bad Reason' has produced atheism. Without doubt, atheism is one of the principal reasons for the unstable conditions existing in the world today. But that was not all the 'Age of Bad Reason' produced. There is another class of people in the world who are just as unreasonable as the atheists. While they seem to differ from the atheists in doctrine, nevertheless they arrive at substantially the same conclusions so far as their attitude toward religion is concerned. These people are called 'agnostics,' and the doctrine which they defend is called 'agnosticism.'

THE MEANING OF 'AGNOSTIC.' The word 'agnostic' is a combination of two words taken from the Greek language, and its meaning is 'one who does not know.' This word was coined in 1869 by Thomas Huxley, the English scientist. He did not intend to designate by the word a person who maintains that the human mind cannot know *anything,* for the word 'skeptic' was already in good use to describe persons such as these. By an agnostic Huxley understood one who claimed that it was impossible for the human mind to arrive at any knowledge concerning God. Asked whether or not God exists, the agnostic would reply: "I do not know, and there is simply no way in which I can ever find out." And since the agnostic refuses to accept the possibility of being certain about the *existence* of God, it necessarily follows that he refuses to accept anything that may be said concerning the *nature* and *attributes* of God. The agnostic does not deny that God exists. His position is that we know nothing on this subject. God in his opinion is so completely outside the pale of human experience and so incomprehensible to the human intellect that we can neither affirm nor deny anything in His regard.

Herbert Spencer, another English scientist, who lived from 1820 to 1903, was a still greater exponent of agnosticism than was Huxley. The meaning which he attached to agnosticism, however, was somewhat different. Spencer did not deny the existence of God. On the contrary, he admitted that God did exist, and spoke of Him as 'a power which the universe manifests.' But this power, he said, is so great and the human mind is so small that it is impossible for a man to know anything about God. Spencer, in fact, called Him 'The Unknowable.' To Spencer the mighty forces of the universe were a clear proof that somewhere, hidden from mortal eyes, is a great power from which in some way emanates all the power and beauty of the world. But is this power a person? Is it a power possessed of wisdom, goodness, and love? Does it act with a purpose, and is it possible for us to discover what that purpose is? To all these questions Spencer would answer in the negative.

AGNOSTICISM ILLOGICAL. If God is indeed unknowable, either as claimed by Huxley or as claimed by Spencer, it must be for one of two reasons: (1) because we cannot know anything which we do not perceive by means of our senses, or (2) because we cannot know anything about the infinite. But neither one of these reasons is logical or valid.

It is not true that we can know nothing which we do not perceive through our senses. Take, for example, radio waves. No one has ever seen, heard, felt, or tasted them. Programs are being transmitted at all hours of the day and night, and the air at all times is literally full of radio waves. They are not only near you—they actually pass through your body; and yet you do not perceive them by any of your senses. You perceive their *effects,* and from the effects you reason to the existence of the waves.

Oftentimes you know that someone is your friend—that he likes you. From his looks, words, or actions you arrive at the knowledge that a certain feeling exists in his mind and heart. You do not see the feeling, yet you know it is there.

All human knowledge does indeed begin with the senses, but we constantly use our reason to arrive at a further knowledge of things that are themselves invisible. Therefore the fact that God is invisible does not make it impossible for us to know that He exists.

Furthermore, the fact that God is infinite while we are finite does not make Him completely unknowable. At least we know that God exists and that He must be most wise and powerful to have been able to create the world. And there are many other things that we can learn if we only look closely enough. A little child is very insignificant in comparison with the Pope; but when the Pope in an audience gives his blessing to little children, they know at least something about him. So we, who are insignificant in comparison with God, can know that God is our superior, that we are dependent upon Him for everything, and that we should therefore be willing to obey and serve Him. You can easily see that agnosticism makes us even lower than the brute animal, for a dog knows something at least about his master, while agnosticism says that man can know nothing at all about his master, God. So agnosticism is not only unreasonable, but also untrue; we can know at least something about God.

AGNOSTICISM MOST HARMFUL. Agnosticism is not only unreasonable; it also has very bad effects on the life of the soul. It can well be termed *the lazy man's doctrine,* for it is founded upon the principle, "I can't." This is simply a lazy man's attitude. How many home runs would a baseball player make if every time he came into the batter's box he were to think, "I can't hit it"? What progress would science have made if every scientist were infected with "I can't" every time he was confronted with a difficulty? Had science taken the lazy, indifferent attitude of the agnostic, the world would still be suffering from diseases and epidemics of diseases that are now controllable. Now, it is important to preserve life for the body, but it is far more important to preserve the life of the soul. The agnostic refuses to try to learn what God wishes us to do. If he were willing to make the effort, he could discover many things about God, about virtue and vice, about life in the next world. He refuses even to think about these things, and so he is like a man who starves because he will not go to the pantry to get food.

ARE THERE AGNOSTICS TODAY? There are many practical agnostics in the world today. It is not, however, because they really understand what agnosticism is, but because it offers a convenient excuse for their irregular lives. Not everybody who calls himself an agnostic is really such. A great many self-styled agnostics hardly know what agnosticism means. They oftentimes make that claim to cover up a bad will. With many of the self-styled agnostics their agnosticism is based on the principle: "I do not want to know"; to them, agnosticism is a vague term that provides them with an excuse for refusing to think about the salvation of their souls. Such a branch of agnosticism is nothing more than practical atheism.

AGNOSTICISM LEADS TO ATHEISM. Agnosticism, in the real meaning of the term, is not atheistic. However, it leads to practical atheism. It does not deny God's existence, but does deny man's ability to know anything about God. What is the logical result of such a doctrine? Let us suppose that there is a vein of gold hidden in the heart of a mountain and known only to you. Of what value would that knowledge be to you if you thought it was beyond anybody's power to reach it? The knowledge would be valueless, and the gold you would never possess. As far as practical results are concerned, you might just as well deny that you ever knew of the gold. And so it is with the agnostic: he might just as well deny God's existence, for in practice it amounts to the same thing.

MILD AGNOSTICS AND RELIGIOUS INDIFFERENTISTS. There are a great many real agnostics in the world today. We may find them among men of science, who are sometimes inclined to say that God is completely outside the sphere of our experience and that in consequence we can know nothing concerning Him. And probably one out of every ten persons whom you pass on the street is what we might call a mild agnostic. A mild agnostic is one who does not claim that we can know nothing about God, but who maintains that we can know nothing with absolute certainty. In his opinion, anything we say concerning God is

possibly true, or is leading us *closer to the truth,* but it is not certainly, positively, and unchangeably true. The mild agnostic is apt to be an indifferentist; that is, he does not cling to any one faith and consider all others wrong, but he is *indifferent* in regard to religious beliefs, considering that all contain something that is good, and that it is impossible to say with certainty that any one of them is wholly correct. The mild agnostic may be a church-goer, but he selects from among the things he learns in church certain ones which catch his fancy, rejecting the others. His creed is summed up in the words: "After all, it does not matter what we believe, as long as we play the game squarely and do our best." He does not claim that we can know nothing about God, but he feels that we have not learned anything definite as yet. He thinks a bit about the subject, for to do so gives him a certain peace of heart; and he hopes that his thinking and that of others may bring mankind closer to truth at some time in the future.

Modern Protestantism is a soil ideally suited to the production of mild agnostics. You will meet them everywhere you go. Every chapter in this book is meant as an argument against them.

POINTS FOR REVIEW AND DISCUSSION

1. What is agnosticism? Who is its founder?

2. How does agnosticism lead to atheism?

3. How does agnosticism affect the life of the soul?

4. Which do agnostics really attack, God's existence or God's rights?

5. Why is the agnostic attitude lacking in reverence and humility?

6. Mention some great minds whose absorbing ambition was to know more about God.

7. Comment on the mild agnosticism in this statement: "The only thing that really matters is to love our common Father and our fellow men." Where is the agnosticism in the statement? What else *does* matter? Why?

THE NEXT LESSON

The previous lessons, in which the existence of God was established by arguments derived from reason, laid stress on God's intelligence, infinite power, and eternity. We now wish to examine more closely into another attribute of God: His loving interest in each one of His creatures. This will be the subject of the next lesson.

CHAPTER TEN

THE PERSONAL GOD

HAT IS A PERSONAL GOD? Non-Catholics who are naturally good and religious frequently ask: "Do you believe in a personal God?" There is something pathetic in this question. Those who ask it feel the need for God and desire to know God, but have only a very vague idea of what God is like. What do they really mean when they ask whether there is a personal God? Could God be *impersonal?* What is a personal God?

There is no need for us to give here that definition of 'person' which we might find in a textbook on psychology. We know well enough what we mean by a personal God. We mean a God who is intelligent, who has power, who acts with a purpose and possesses wisdom in carrying out that purpose, and above all who is interested in each one of His creatures as a mother is interested in her children. This is what we mean by a personal God.

Perhaps we have already said enough to prove that God is a personal God; if so, let us at least set it before our eyes again in a different light so that no doubt may ever trouble us again.

GOD ACTS FOR A PURPOSE. God in creating the universe must have had a purpose or end in view. Reason proves the truth of this statement. When you see a number of workmen begin to unload tools and materials from trucks and start to work, you know that they must have a purpose, a plan. Anyone who spends time and money on a piece of work has some purpose in mind. If God, then, had made the world without a purpose, He would not have been intelligent, for He would have done something without having a purpose in doing it.

Hence we know with certainty that God must have had a purpose in creating the universe. The question then arises: What was that purpose?

FIRST PURPOSE OF CREATION. Now, before this universe was made, only God existed. He could not, then, have created the universe for anybody else, for there *was* nobody else. Nor could God have created the universe purely for the sake of the living creatures who would inhabit that universe. God, the Infinite One, is the center toward which all else must turn. It would be unworthy of God for Him to permit creatures to be the only or even the first purpose in His mind. Therefore God must have created the universe for Himself.

But God is perfect. He is not wanting in anything; He has all that He needs. But there is one thing which God did not *need,* but which nevertheless He did not have, and that was the praise, honor, and love of creatures possessing intelligence. This is what we call God's *external* glory as opposed to that *internal* glory which He had within Himself from all eternity. This external glory was His first purpose in creation. This reasoning is in harmony with the Bible when it says: "The Lord hath made all things for Himself" (Proverbs 16:4), and, "Everyone that calleth upon My name, I have created him for My glory" (Isaias 43:7).

SECOND PURPOSE OF CREATION. But how was this external glory to come about? Could trees and rocks give external glory to God? No; God might have filled the entire universe with objects such as these, and not a particle of external glory would have come to Him. They would have stood there—silent and unresponsive. There would have been no sufficient purpose for creating them.

Who, then, can give external glory to God? Only free and intelligent creatures who, seeing His glory and goodness, offer Him honor, praise, and love. But before they can do this they must share in some way in His happiness. They must not be like a mob of conquered slaves cheering some despot while they hate him in their hearts. They must praise God freely because He has been so good to them. Therefore God's second purpose in creation was the happiness of His creatures.

God's nature is such that He could not desire anything but *happy* creatures. How can we ever forget a thought as beautiful as this?

GOD'S POWER AND WISDOM IN CREATION. God, therefore, out of His goodness and unselfishness, created the universe so that creatures might enjoy some of His happiness. But God could not have done this if He were merely *good*. There must be other powers used to carry out that plan. If things are to enjoy happiness, it is necessary first to bring them into existence. This must be done by the omnipotence or all-powerfulness of God. Moreover, when the things are created, they need to be directed and guided toward that happiness, otherwise they can never reach the end for which they were intended. Hence God must call upon His *wisdom* so to direct things that they partake of His happiness.

When God was creating things in the universe, His wisdom must have prompted Him to make everything most carefully in order that His plan might be carried out successfully. Everything must be made in just such a way that it would act in harmony with everything else, otherwise His plan would be defeated. God, then, had to give His personal supervision to every minute detail so that success would follow. We see in the affairs of men how such care is necessary. Personal supervision is always necessary to assure success. When Sir Malcolm Campbell was building his speed car to beat his record of 270 miles an hour, every nut and bolt received his personal attention. If everything did not act perfectly and in harmony with everything else, failure would be the inevitable result. Before Lindbergh crossed the Atlantic, his plane, called "The Spirit of St. Louis," received a most minute personal supervision. So God in making His universe must have had a personal care over everything that was to be in it. In summarizing, then, what

"*In a moment of indignation have I hid My face a little while from thee . . . but with everlasting kindness have I had mercy on thee*" (Isaias 54:8).

reason teaches us concerning the purpose of God, we find that God must use His omnipotent power to make the universe and that He must call upon His wisdom in so creating it as to make it fulfill His purpose.

But did God actually do this? In order to answer this question, we must first look at the universe to see if we can find the omnipotence and wisdom of God in it.

There is no difficulty about seeing God's omnipotence, for we have proved that the universe was created. But to create —to make something out of nothing—requires more than finite power. God's omnipotence, then, must have been used.

Is there evidence of God's wisdom in the universe? To see this properly, again let us look at the universe. To the uneducated mind the universe looks like a great tangled mass of innumerable things that do not fit together and do not seem to have any connection with one another. But we have already seen how in all these things there is constant evidence of a wonderful design.

GOD'S SPECIAL CARE OF MAN. It will be noticed that all things in the world are of two classes: those that have an intellect and can understand; those that lack an intellect and cannot understand. When God created things that were without intellects He *forced* them into doing what was necessary to make His plan a success. This force which God uses is manifested in the physical laws. In the physical laws we can see God's personal supervision. Let us take the sun, for example. The sun was made to give light and heat to the world. If the sun gave too much or too little heat or light to the world, it would destroy all life in the world.

But the sun does not give too much or too little; it acts perfectly. Now the sun, not having an intellect, cannot direct its own acts. So, consequently, God must have given it His personal supervision when He made it so that it *would* always work perfectly. We can say the same about everything else in the unreasoning world.

Did God give any personal attention to those having an intellect? Man is the only being on earth in this class, and it is with man that God has shown a most personal relationship. A study of man, in comparison with other creatures, will show that this is true. It was the goodness of God which prompted Him to make someone who would share His happiness, and man was chosen for that honor. Now, to share God's happiness is to know and to love God. Consequently God provided man with a reasoning faculty so that it would be possible for man to know Him. God wanted man's love to come freely. No one wants or enjoys another's love if that love be forced; love to be true love *must* be free. So God provided man with a faculty of free will, so that man might freely love Him. What personal care, then, must God have had when He made man! No other creature on earth has such faculties. Indeed, He must have loved man when He gave man so much!

Now, God must have loved every one of us, for He gave to all men individually the same faculties of knowing and loving Him. Since God has been so kind and generous to all men, it would be unreasonable for any individual to think that there is not a personal bond of affection between God and himself. "He made the little and the great, and He hath equally care of all" (Wisdom 6:8). "The very hairs of your head are all numbered" (Matthew 10:30).

POINTS FOR REVIEW AND DISCUSSION

1. Why must God have had a purpose in creating?

2. What was His first purpose? His second purpose?

3. How can inanimate and unintelligent beings, such as trees and animals, give glory to God?

4. Was wisdom required in creation? Was omnipotence required in creation?

5. How does God direct beings that have no intellect? How does He direct those that have an intellect?

6. Is grace a means of guidance? Why do we say nothing of it here?

7. If God wishes only happy creatures, how do you explain the existence of hell? How can souls in hell give that kind of glory to God which we say He desires?

8. How can you say that God wishes us to love Him freely when He forces us to love Him by threatening us with hell?

9. Discuss which of the following are essential to a *person,* and prove that God possesses them: (1) Power to know. (2) A human voice. (3) Power to will. (4) Power to act. (5) A father and a mother. (6) A certain color of hair. (7) Power to love, as a result of knowledge and will.

10. Discuss whether or not it follows from all this that God is our Father.

11. The Protestant author George Herbert Betts, in his book on the teaching of religion, writes as follows:

"It is at this point [that is, in regard to God's personality] that the modern man has the greatest difficulty about God. He would like to believe that God has personality of which his own personality is a faint reflection, but he hesitates and is uncertain. He thinks of God as Creative Energy, as Dynamic Law, as the Ultimate, as an Order of Existence, or some other impersonal agency. He does not see how these cold abstractions can stand for anything warm and personal such as one finds in a friend who is able to understand us, love us, pity us, rejoice with us."

a. What statement made in this chapter is supported by this quotation from Mr. Betts?

b. Do you think that his statement fits Protestants whom you know?

c. Complete the following sentence as an answer to the difficulty described in the quotation: "God is truly a person because . . ."

THE NEXT LESSON

The next lesson will deal with the providence of God, by which we understand God's way of bringing about those loving purposes which we have seen He has in regard to man.

CHAPTER ELEVEN

THE PROVIDENCE OF GOD

GOD CREATED THE UNIVERSE. One of the first principles which we learned from reason was the principle of causality. This principle stated that every effect must have a cause. When we applied this principle to the universe we found that the universe and everything in it must have a cause, and we called that cause God. God, then, is the First Cause of the universe. The act by which God caused the world to come into existence was the act of creation. God created the world, producing it from nothing by an act of His divine will. That point has been very definitely settled and must be believed by anyone using his reason properly.

CREATION INCLUDES PROVIDENCE. Again, if we use our reason, we will find that the act of creating could not have been the only act of God in making the universe. In our arguments for the existence of God we concluded from the existence of law in the universe that God must have been an *intelligent* being. Hence the act of creation came from a supremely intelligent mind. Now, if God is supremely intelligent and created the world, our reason tells us He must have had a motive or purpose in creating the universe. No man does anything unless he has a purpose in doing it. In order to be considered intelligent, a man must be able to point to some purpose for doing what he does; otherwise he is looked upon as insane. Consequently it is only reasonable to suppose that God had a purpose in creating the world.

But in order to have any purpose succeed, it is necessary to draw up a method of procedure; that is, to work out ways and means of making that purpose do what it was intended to do. This method of procedure, or the ways and means of obtaining the purpose intended, is nothing more than a *plan.* Hence if a purpose is to be worth anything, a plan must be devised by which the purpose is carried into execution. Every man must have a plan in mind when he has an intention of doing anything. If he wants to build a house and has the purpose of building it to live in it in comfort, he will draw up such a plan as will accomplish his purpose, so that when the house is built it will be just what he intended it to be. We can say from reason that God used the same method in creating the universe. He had a purpose, as we have said, in creating the world, and consequently must have had a plan for carrying out that purpose. To deny this would be to deny intelligence in God.

Instead of using the word *plan,* let us substitute the word *providence.* After all, that is just what providence means.

Providence, a word coming from the Latin language, means *the act of foreseeing.* And every plan is an act of foreseeing, for to plan means to look ahead and determine what is necessary in order to gain the purpose intended. Certainly, then, if God had intelligence—and we know this to be true—He must have looked ahead to determine ways and means of accomplishing His purpose of creating the world. God, therefore, must have had providence in creating the universe.

NATURE OF GOD'S PROVIDENCE. But in what does this providence of God consist? Where shall we find it? Again let us use our reason. In order that God's purpose in creating the world be accomplished, it is necessary that God should continue to keep in existence the things which He made until their purpose is fulfilled. Were He at any moment to withdraw His support, nothing could exist, nothing could act, but everything would return to the nothingness from which it came. At every moment, then, God is, so to speak, thinking of His creatures and conferring on them the help they need to exist and to act. For since creatures have no power to *bring* themselves into existence, it follows that they have no power to *keep* themselves in existence. God must will that they should *continue* to exist, just as He had to will that they should *begin* to exist. This is the first result of His providence, and is called God's *concurrence.*

But it is not enough that things should exist; they must be directed toward the end for which God wished them to exist. Hence *everything* in the universe was *so created* that

*The marvels of our age are due to thoughtful planning.
. . . Is the all-wise God inferior to man? Did He fashion
this great universe without a purpose or a goal?*

it would assist in fulfilling God's intention. If this were not true and things did not assist in carrying out God's plan, God would have been unwise in creating them—they would only defeat His purpose. Hence everything that God created must be directed toward the perfection of God's plan. But law is what directs a thing toward its perfection. God in His providence created a law for everything, so that everything He created might accomplish His purpose. God assumed the rôle of lawgiver, and His laws are spoken of as His government of the world. Providence, then, includes both the plan of the universe in the mind of God, and the ways and means —God's constant support and His laws—which He employs to govern the universe so that the purpose which He had in mind may be accomplished.

Everything in the world, then, must live up to laws, otherwise God's purpose will not be accomplished. God in His providence worked out a plan by which they *would* live up to law, for God was not to be defeated in His intention. Consequently He made two sets of laws: one governing creatures without reason and a second governing creatures with reason. For the creatures not having reason He created the physical laws—laws that *forced* them to act in such a way that God might realize His purpose. That is why a stone always falls to the earth; it is *forced* to act as God intended it to act. That is why the animal instinctively acts as it does; although the dog, for example, may not be literally forced to do everything that it does, its life in general is governed by strong instinctive tendencies which cannot be resisted. But for creatures with reason—man is the only one on earth coming under this head—it was different. God made a law for him which is called the moral law, but he did not force man into obeying it. He gave man intelligence by which he could see and understand God's purpose in creating the world, and He gave him a free will by which he could follow the law or not. But of what use would it have been to make known a law if man were left without a strong motive for observing the law? We can therefore conclude that there must be in God's plan some system of rewards and punishments. These rewards and punishments are what we call the *sanctions* of the law, and they also are a result of God's providence; they are a necessary part of His plan for the intelligent creation and government of the world.

Finally, since God in His infinite intelligence always knows everything that is happening on earth, and since in His love He has a special care for all His creatures, our reason tells us that He may be expected sometimes to interfere for the purpose of causing His will to be carried out. If physical forces, such as sickness or famine, threaten injury to His creatures, or if the free actions of men are resulting in harm, He may exercise His supreme power and wisdom to avert the evil. He will do so whenever it seems to Him advisable, and He will do so more readily if we have appealed to Him as our Father for help.

In short, God is so infinitely wise, powerful, and good that it would be impossible for Him to permit mere chance or the sinful will of man to govern His universe. He has a plan, and He does what is necessary to have that plan carried out. This is what we mean by the providence of God.

POINTS FOR REVIEW AND DISCUSSION

1. Prove that God must have had a purpose in creating the world.

2. What does providence mean?

3. Show how God's constant support of all His creatures in existence, His physical laws, His moral law, the sanctions of the moral law, and His readiness to hear our prayers are part of His providence.

4. What might you expect of God's providence if:
   a. A storm threatens to spoil your picnic.
   b. Sickness threatens your father's life.
   c. You are trying to decide upon your vocation.

5. Prove that one who fully understands God's providence can never fear and never complain.

6. Explain why God does not have to change His design or purpose when He hears and grants our prayers or when He works a miracle.

THE NEXT LESSON

If God is as good and loving as we say, why is there so much evil in the world? This question merits special attention and will be taken up in the next lesson.

CHAPTER TWELVE

THE PROBLEM OF EVIL

PROBLEM CREATED BY THE EVIL IN THE WORLD. When we were treating of providence we found that God, as an intelligent being, had a purpose in creating the world. Reason also told us that, as God had a purpose in mind, He must have had also a plan in mind by which He could work out that purpose. Now, of course, it is impossible for us to look into the mind of God and see just what that plan was. If there is any way of knowing God's mind, it can only be by observing the work God performed. He created the universe, and it is the universe, then, that must give us some knowledge of God and the plan God had in mind. An examination of the product gives us, in some degree, a knowledge of the mind of the producer. And so when we look at the workings of nature and its laws, we can know in some manner the plan that was in the mind of God when He created it.

But here is where a difficulty arises. We know that God is intelligent, good, and just; He could not be otherwise and still be God. Everything, then, that He does must always be wise, good, and just. Yet when we take a casual glance at nature and its workings, there seem to be imperfection in nature and disorder in its workings. When we consider the existence of tornadoes, cyclones, earthquakes, famine, pestilence, diseases, murders, lies, the oppression of the poor by the rich and powerful, and other such distressing things, it would appear that the world lacks the perfection and order which we would expect in something produced by a God who is provident, wise, good, and just. This lack of order and perfection is described by the general term 'evil.'

That there is evil in the world is certain. To deny it would be to deny everyday experience. We see it every day on every side. But God created this universe, and is He not responsible for everything in it? Shall we, therefore, attribute this lack of perfection and order to God? Or, in other words, is God to blame for the presence of evil in the world?

FALSE EXPLANATIONS OF EVIL. This question of evil has been a great stumbling block to many minds from the very earliest times. In ancient times the presence of evil in the world led men to believe that there were two gods— a good god and a god of evil. The Manichaeans held this theory, and it is still held today in some parts of the world. Others deny that God has any providence over the world, and say that He simply permits anything at all to happen. Finally, in both ancient and modern times evil has been a basic reason for the denial of the existence of God, and has afforded an excellent excuse to many to live lives of practical atheism.

There can be no doubt that the presence of evil is a serious problem. Cardinal Newman considered it the greatest and the most perplexing of all problems. Nevertheless, we are able to solve this problem at least to the extent of seeing that the presence of evil in the world is not opposed to the wisdom and goodness of God.

TWO KINDS OF EVIL. If we look at the various kinds of evil and attempt to classify them, we will find that all evils may be reduced to two kinds: physical evils and moral evils. Physical evils are the disorders and imperfections of physical nature, such as cyclones, tornadoes, pain, and things of the same kind. Moral evils are disorders and imperfections of the moral law, such as lies, murders, thefts, and so forth. We may classify all evils of the moral order under the general term of sin.

PHYSICAL EVIL. Now, there is no doubt that what we call physical disorders exist. There are apparent physical imperfections everywhere in nature. If these imperfections were *wholly bad,* God could not be their author. But if they are things that produce good results, although perhaps in an imperfect or disagreeable manner, then God can be their author. God makes everything perfectly, not in the sense that nothing has any limitation or lack of absolute perfection, but in the sense that everything is perfectly adapted to that end which God had in view.

Let us take the physical evil of pain. Is pain a thing that is entirely evil? On the contrary, is pain not productive of good? How would we ever know what was wrong with us if it were not for pain? A cavity in a tooth causes pain, yet if it were not for that pain we would never be aware of a decaying tooth, and a decaying tooth would not only cause ruin to itself but would eventually ruin every tooth in the mouth. Pain is not wholly evil, but is nature's warning of something wrong in the system. So it is with earthquakes, tornadoes, and other such things. They are but nature's method of cleaning house, of throwing off at various times forces which, if not dispelled but allowed to collect, would eventually bring ruin upon the whole world and everybody in it.

"I now see," you may say, "that earthquakes and sickness are not evil in the sense that they are bad from every point of view. I see that they are productive of some good, and that as a consequence God could be the cause of them. But if He is so wise and good, why did He not arrange to produce the same results in ways that did not cause us trouble and pain?"

To demand this is to demand that God should give His creatures, not only a *great* gift, but a *perfect* gift. It is to ask for life without being willing to pay any price for life. And we have also seen that creatures were made for the purpose of giving glory to God, and we shall see later how great a reward is promised to those who are faithful in doing what God wishes. But if pain and weariness, suffering and sorrow, did not exist, we would not have the same opportunity of doing great things for God and of meriting an equally great reward. Patience, courage, brotherly helpfulness, and many other virtues which we most admire would be far less frequently exercised in a world free from physical evil.

MORAL EVIL. As for evils in the moral order, God in no way can be held responsible for them. A moral evil is nothing more than a violation of the moral law. If the moral law is violated, it is man who is the cause. Not only did God give man a free will, but He also gave him an intellect by which he might know how to use that free will. If man does not use his intellect properly and allows his free will to violate the moral law, it is man who is to be held responsible, not God. Hence in the moral order we cannot hold God responsible in any way for evil. God merely permits the sin. He does not wish it to exist. But He wishes man to give Him glory and to merit heaven by choosing not to sin when he might choose to sin. And man does sometimes choose to sin, but even from this sin God can make good result.

In one of his poems Robert Browning describes a beautiful and apparently holy young girl who was really a thief. When she died her hair was found full of stolen gold pieces which she had hidden there. From this the poet argued that there must be some sort of corruption in human nature.

What we are endeavoring to do in this book is to build up the truth of Catholicism on the foundation of reason. Therefore we will not appeal to revelation at this point. But we may at least ask a question suggested by the fact that man, the most perfect of creatures, suffers most of all from evil of every kind. It is this: Does not this evil suggest that man may have committed some wrong which caused

If from the greatest sin of all time . . . the unjust cruci-fixion of our Lord . . . God made so great good to flow . . . can we doubt that "to them that love God all things work together unto good" (Romans 8:28)?

God to scourge him? Is it not possible that the evil which we see was not part of God's original plan? And if it was something added to the original plan, must we not believe, since we know that God is wholly good, that it was added for the purpose of bringing about certain beneficial results which God knows better than we?

Is it not folly for us to think that we know *all* that is in the mind of God? God's mind is infinitely great; man's mind is small. That God has a plan or providence for the world is certain, but just exactly what that plan is in every detail is impossible to know with a mind as small as ours. Is it not presumptuous and unreasonable on our part to deny the whole plan and providence of God just because we do not know *all* of it? If we could easily understand everything that God does, we would be His mental equals. Precisely because He is infinite and we are finite, some of His decrees must be difficult to understand. And so the problem of evil remains a problem. But our reason has convinced us of this: No evil that we see is proof that a wise and all-good God does not exist.

POINTS FOR REVIEW AND DISCUSSION

1. What argument do enemies of God build up from the existence of evil?

2. Mention three false explanations of the existence of evil.

3. Describe two kinds of evil and explain why God can cause the first and permit the second.

4. Suggest how God **can** make good result from sin.

5. Prove that the history of Judas Iscariot is not an argument against the providence of God.

FAITH AND REASON

6. The non-Christian writer Walter Lippmann speaks of evil as follows:

"The greatest of all perplexities in theology has been to reconcile the infinite goodness of God with his omnipotence. Nothing puts a greater strain on the faith of the common man than the existence of utterly irrational suffering in the universe, and the problem which tormented Job still troubles every devout and thoughtful man who beholds the monstrous injustices of nature. If there were no pain in the world except that which was felt by responsible beings who had knowingly transgressed some law of conduct, there would, of course, be no problem of evil. Pain would be nothing but a rational punishment. But the pain which is suffered by those who according to all human standards are innocent, by children and by animals, for example, cannot be fitted into any rational theory of reward and punishment."

    a. If what Mr. Lippmann says is true, what would follow concerning either the existence or the nature of God?

    b. Is it wrong for God to create beings capable of suffering? Would it be wrong for Him to demand one hour of pain for every hour of happy, pleasurable life?

    c. Is reward and punishment the only purpose that suffering may serve? Can it increase merit? Can it give others an opportunity of practicing virtue? Can it help to teach all men that earth is not their final home?

    d. What is your general opinion of the passage quoted?

THE NEXT LESSON

We have now completed our study of the nature of God. What else is necessary if we wish to serve Him as He desires? It is this, that we should also understand our own nature. What we can and should do for God depends upon what we are. In the next lesson, then, we will turn our attention to ourselves.

CHAPTER THIRTEEN

THE NATURE OF
THE SOUL

EN ARE CONVINCED THAT THEY HAVE SOULS. For many years you have been convinced that you have a soul, and in holding this conviction you are in agreement with the vast majority of men. We believe that we have souls, that these souls are what give us life, that our souls remain essentially the same from the beginning to the end of life, that it is the separation of the soul from the body that causes death, and that after death the soul will continue to live. Even primitive men believed these things many centuries ago. In this lesson and the next we wish to prove these facts, so that we may be prepared to meet the arguments of those who deny the existence of the soul.

We learn what the soul is by reasoning from what we see in man. As explained in a previous lesson, an effect tells us something about the cause which produced it. If we put our hand in a lighted oven, we know that there is some cause present which has the power of producing heat. If we put our hand in a refrigerator, we know that there is some cause present which has the power of producing cold. There must be some cause in man for the things which we see man do. Let us see what man is and what he does, and from this we will learn something about man's soul.

MAN IS A LIVING BEING. The first thing we observe in man is that he is a living being. A rock on a mountainside remains in the same position century after century. The force of gravity may cause it to roll down the mountain, moss may grow on it, or the moisture in the air may cause it to crack and crumble, but in itself and of itself it can do nothing. But the small seed which falls from the mother plant upon the earth germinates and grows into a plant, and in time produces seeds which give rise to new plants. The seed has a power which the rock does not have. It can do things of itself. It is *living*.

Man is not like a barrel which has no feeling and which remains in one place unless somebody moves it. He can feel, he can move, he can freely choose this thing or that. But every effect must have its cause, and therefore man must have something which makes him alive.

MAN'S MENTAL LIFE. This life of which we have spoken shows itself in many ways, as, for example, in digesting one's food and converting it into one's own substance, in breathing, in the circulation of the blood, and in many similar ways. But what we wish to study here is man's *mental life*—his knowledge, his thought, his free will. In this mental life we may note three things:

You cannot see the hatred in the tyrant's heart . . . you cannot see the love that fills the martyr's soul. But invisible things may be most real . . . and we can be certain that they exist.

FAITH AND REASON

1. You are able at this moment to tell what you mean by such things as virtue, patriotism, beauty, piety, God, and so forth. These are real things, but they can not be seen, touched, or heard. That is why they are called *immaterial* things. We are able to *know* these immaterial things. This is the first thing we observe about man's mind.

2. Moreover, we are able to *reason* about things. What do we mean by reasoning? We mean the process of arriving at some new truth by thinking about truths already known. For example, manufacturers of automobiles are constantly striving to develop a motor which will give more miles to a gallon of gasoline. They employ engineers who study the known facts concerning motors, and who finally *reason* that, if a certain thing is done, a certain result will follow. Everywhere in the world we see the effects of man's reasoning. Imagine for a moment that you are boys and girls of the fifth century before Christ instead of living as you do in the twentieth century after Christ. Would you have automobiles, airplanes, motion pictures, elevators, railroads, steamships, and a thousand other similar inventions? And, lest we get the bad habit of thinking that all mankind's advances have been in these material things, you would not have been taught, five centuries before Christ, the same attitude toward art, literature, citizenship, and recreation that you are taught today. All these improvements came about because man is able to reason.

The lower animals cannot reason in this way. We were speaking of boys and girls who lived five centuries before Christ. Five centuries before Christ some of the pyramids of Egypt were almost thirty centuries old. When we unearth these pyramids from the sands of the desert, we find spider webs in them. Perhaps these spider webs were not made fully fifty centuries ago, but they were certainly made very far back in the past. Are the spider webs of today made any better than those old ones? Have spiders (one of the most intelligent of the lower animals) made the slightest improvement in anything they do? No; neither they nor any other lower animal ever makes any progress. Why not? Because they cannot think—they cannot reason.

All that we can do to train animals is to get them to acquire some rather simple habit by using rewards and punishments. If animals, possessing as they do superior speed and strength, could really reason, they would very soon kill off the entire human race. Men trap animals, but animals do not trap men. Man's reason makes him the ruler of the animal kingdom.

3. Finally, man has the gift of *free will*. He is free to do what he wishes. Confronted with two alternatives, he can choose this one or that one. Now, an act of the will is an immaterial thing. Why is it immaterial? Because it does not depend upon matter. Matter is any extended object like a loaf of bread, a tree, or anything else that occupies space. Certain acts *depend upon matter for their very existence*. For example, when a cat smells a saucer of milk and goes to drink it, what happens is that a material thing (a saucer of milk) produces an effect upon other material things (the nerves and the brain of the cat). But what happens when, for example, you say to yourself: "I will make an act of

thanksgiving to God for His mercy to me"? When you say such a thing, you first of all *know* something which never could be seen, heard, felt, or touched; you *know* that the invisible God has been merciful to you because he has permitted you to live in spite of your sins and infidelities. Secondly, you make an act of the will which is also invisible and immaterial; it does not occupy any space, it is not at all like a loaf of bread or a saucer of milk.

SUMMARY. What have we learned so far? We have learned (1) that there is something in man which makes him a living being, (2) that man can know immaterial things, (3) that man can reason, developing new truths from old truths, (4) that man can make acts of the will, and (5) that these acts are immaterial, proving the existence of something in man which is likewise immaterial.

We call this immaterial thing the soul, and we say that it is *spiritual,* for we use the word 'spiritual' to describe a *living thing* which has activities that are not material. This soul of yours is independent of other souls, for you know that it is *your* soul, not mine or anybody else's, which acts within you. This soul of yours is permanent, for the fact that you recognize and accept as *your* acts things which you did years and years ago proves that one and the same soul has resided in you all that time. This soul of yours needs the body in order that it may act, but it needs the body only as an instrument, just as the organist needs the organ if he is to play.

EACH SOUL SEPARATELY CREATED. It is not an argument against God's all-powerfulness to say that He cannot do things which are contradictory in themselves. God cannot make a square circle, for nothing can be a circle and a square at the same time. God cannot make irrational animals which are rational; He could have made horses and dogs rational had He wished to do so, but as long as they are irrational, they cannot be rational at the same time.

So, likewise, God cannot give to purely material things the power to produce immaterial results. If they can produce immaterial results, they cannot be purely material. A lilac bush has no power to think, for it is a purely material and irrational thing. Possibly God could give it the power to think, even without a brain and a central nervous system, but then it would cease to be purely material and irrational.

The human body is formed from the body of the mother, and this is a material thing. What of the soul, which makes the body living? It does not seem possible that God should give to the material body of the mother the power to produce the immaterial soul, and therefore we hold that each human soul is individually created by God.

An atheistic professor in a medical school once turned to his class as he was working on a dead body, and said with a sneer: "Can any of you show me a soul here?" This is the attitude of many unbelievers today. They cannot *see* the soul, and so they say that it does not exist. But who has ever seen ether, that invisible substance which fills up every bit of space in the universe? Nobody has ever seen or felt it, yet we know that it exists. If at this moment all the ether were to be destroyed, the heat and light of the sun could no longer reach us. In an instant the world would be plunged into darkness more profound than that of the darkest night, and the temperature would go down to absolute zero. In that instant every vestige of life upon earth would be destroyed, just as if the world had been sprayed from end to end with a giant torch of fiery flame.

Nobody has ever seen ether, but we know that it exists. Nobody has ever seen a soul, yet we know that souls exist. They *must* exist, for otherwise there would be no efficient cause for the things which we know that man can do. Thus reason has given us a solid argument for a thing which we have always accepted as a fact.

POINTS FOR REVIEW AND DISCUSSION

1. How should we go about determining the nature of man's soul?

2. Prove that man is living.

3. What three activities of man show that there is something within him which is immaterial?

4. Why do we say that man's soul is spiritual?

5. Answer this objection: "The soul cannot act without the body, and therefore it must be material."

6. Speaking of present-day belief in the soul, Walter Lippmann says:

"The thoroughly modern man has really ceased to believe that there is an immortal essence presiding like a king over his appetites. The word 'soul' has become a figure of speech, which he uses loosely, sometimes to mean his tender aspirations, sometimes to mean the whole collection of his impulses, sometimes, when he is in a hurry, to mean nothing at all."

a. There are more than twenty million Catholics in the United States, all of whom believe in the existence of the soul. Are any of these Catholics as "thoroughly modern" as others are? If so, what is the matter with Mr. Lippmann's first sentence?

b. If man does not have "an immortal essence" (a soul), is there any compelling reason why he should be moral?

c. To what extent do you think Mr. Lippmann is correct in what he says? What ought to be done about the matter?

THE NEXT LESSON

In the next lesson we will ask what happens to the soul after death. Does it cease to exist, or is it immortal?

CHAPTER FOURTEEN

THE IMMORTALITY OF THE SOUL

HE MEANING OF IM-
MORTALITY. To be immortal
means to exist forever, to be imperishable.
When we apply the term to the soul it
means that the soul will have unending
existence, that it is not subject to death.

To know that our soul is immortal is of the greatest consequence to us because it answers the most important question of life. The meaning and purpose of man's existence
have always been looked upon as great and important problems, and the questions: What am I? Why am I? Where
am I going? have been uppermost in the minds of all men
at all times. The doctrine of immortality answers them all
satisfactorily. When man understands that his soul was
created to live forever, life takes on a new aspect. Man real-
izes, then, that he is one of God's chosen creatures, a mas-
terpiece of God's creative hand, modeled after God himself,
and destined to an eternal happiness with his Creator. The
sorrows and disappointments of life—there are many in the

lot of every man—no longer are unbearable, but are borne with patience and fortitude in the hope of an eternal reward. To those who disbelieve or deny this doctrine God becomes a fiction, man is reduced to the level of the brute, morality is but a name, and life itself is meaningless.

IMMORTALITY PROVED FROM REASON. Every doctrine at some time or other has been attacked by someone. The immortality of the soul is no exception, and it, too, has been denied by many, particularly in our own day. Those who deny it base their claim on the theory that there is no distinction between the soul of man and that of the brute animal. We have proved this theory to be false, and hence the denial of immortality, based on this theory, is not to be admitted. There are others who do not actually reject the doctrine of immortality, but who hold that it is impossible to prove it from arguments based on reason. We, on the contrary, in answer to this objection claim that the doctrine of the immortality of the soul, at least so far as the just are concerned, can be proved from reason by (1) the argument from the nature of the soul, (2) the argument from the desire of man, and (3) the argument from the moral order.

THE ARGUMENT FROM THE NATURE OF THE SOUL. The argument from the nature of the soul is used chiefly to show that the soul *can* live without the body. What this means particularly is that the life of the soul does not depend upon the life of the body. If that can be shown, then it will be reasonable to believe that the soul can live on after the death of the body. But is it true that the soul does not depend upon the body for its existence? Yes; for the body, composed as it is of chemical elements, cannot be the reason for the existence of a soul which is immaterial and spiritual. It is true that the soul was created to be united with the body, and that in its activities it uses the assistance of the body. But the soul is a distinct thing, separately created by God, and the fact that it uses the body does not prove that it cannot exist without the body.

When a dog dies, its vital principle ceases to exist, for without the brain and the senses there is nothing that it can do. Consider all the activities that make up the dog's day. It *sees* its master and runs to meet him; it *hears* footsteps, and barks; it *smells* the track of a rabbit, and goes in search of it. It does not have any ideas that are independent of the senses. If, then, its body and senses are taken away there is simply nothing left for the vital principle to do.

It is different with man, for his soul has activities—thinking and willing—for which a body is not essential. Therefore it is evident that the soul of man does not need to cease to exist just because it is separated from the body.

THE SOUL CANNOT DIE. Moreover, death can have no effect upon the existence of the soul. Death is but the separation of a thing into its constituent parts. Death causes man to cease to exist (at least for a time) as man. It does this by bringing about a separation between the two constituent parts of man, his body and his soul. But the soul, as we have shown, is spiritual or immaterial, and what is immaterial is not made up of parts. Man's death, therefore,

In the grave of the loved one they placed arrows for the hunt . . . food for the daily meal . . . mute testimony to that faith in a future life which men of every age have cherished.

does not necessarily imply that his soul will cease to remain in existence.

THE ARGUMENT FROM THE DESIRE FOR HAPPINESS. The desire to be perfectly and permanently happy has been and is the wish of every man. The attainment of happiness is the motive that underlies every human action. This is universally true at all times without exception, and because of this fact, reason tells us that the desire for perfect happiness is in the nature of man. Now, God is the author of nature and upon Him rests the responsibility for creating such a desire in human nature. But reason demands that, since God created such a desire, He must also have created the possibility of fulfilling that desire. For it would be most unjust and unkind of God to have created a wish for something that could never be enjoyed. Would it not be considered most unkind in us to tease a hungry animal with a morsel of food by continually offering it to him, yet never allowing him to have it? But God is most just and kind and loving. Hence if He created the desire in man for happiness, He must have provided some means for man to fulfill and enjoy his desire. It is the conviction and experience of every man that perfect happiness is not attainable in this world. God, then, must allow the souls of the just to live on after the death of the body, so that perfect happiness may be obtained and man's desire be fulfilled. As to the souls of the reprobate, it is certainly not necessary for God to keep them in existence for the reason given here. Whether justice absolutely requires that they should continue to exist in order to suffer the punishment due to their sins is a question into which we need not enter.

THE ARGUMENT FROM THE DEMANDS OF JUSTICE.

Daily experience teaches us that evil men often prosper and that good men often suffer the ills of life. Fact after fact might be cited to show how some men living the life of practical atheists, attentive to the laws neither of God nor of man, apparently meet with much success in this world. On the other hand, there are men who never violate their consciences for the goods and pleasures of this life, and yet misfortune is their lot. It seems, then, that frequently in this life evil men are rewarded and good men punished. This fact is not in accordance with justice. But we know that God is the judge of our merits and that He is infinitely just. Since virtue, then, is not always rewarded in this life nor vice punished, it is most reasonable to believe that there is another life beyond this present world where the justice of God will set straight and make up for the apparent injustice of this life. Hence the immortality of the soul.

POINTS FOR REVIEW AND DISCUSSION

1. What is immortality?
2. Name the three arguments for immortality.
3. Prove immortality from the nature of the soul.
4. Prove immortality from the desire of man.
5. Prove immortality from the moral order.
6. If you were to study biology in a non-Catholic American university, you would almost certainly meet statements like the follow-

ing in your textbook: "Life in man, worm, and plant is essentially the same. Living matter is merely ordinary matter which has assumed, for the time being, a peculiar condition."

    a. Does the author of this statement offer any proof, or does he merely make an assertion? (There is nothing in the entire passage from which the quotation is taken which adds to what is said here.)

    b. How do we determine whether or not life is essentially the same in man, worm, and plant?

    c. If matter is not living, what has to occur before it can 'assume' a peculiar condition?

7. Just as some persons err by saying that we know nothing at all about the condition of the soul after death, so others err by claiming that we can know too much. Criticize the following statement of Charles W. Leadbeater:

"Life after death is no longer a mystery. The world beyond the grave exists under the same natural law as this which we know, and has been explored and examined with scientific accuracy."

THE NEXT LESSON

If man was created by God, and if his soul is spiritual and immortal, what are we to think of the theory of evolution, which teaches that man has developed from some lower form of animal? This question will be discussed in our next lesson.

CHAPTER FIFTEEN

EVOLUTION

HAT IS EVOLUTION? From the viewpoint of theory, evolution declares that all the species of plants and animals now existing upon the earth are modified descendants of earlier forms of life. The changes which are supposed to have resulted in the species which we now see are frequently said to have required 'countless millions of years.' Under this theory, man, many thousands of years ago, evolved from the 'monkey' or anthropoid ape.

This theory, which applies to organic evolution, is the one which is most frequently defended and discussed. In a still broader sense, as proposed by Haeckel, evolution endeavors to explain the appearance of life upon earth by saying that primitive organisms of an extremely simple type evolved through a succession of very slow changes from non-living matter.

The theory of evolution is held very widely in our country. College textbooks are full of references to it. Many scientists treat it as a fact so well established that only the most ignorant man can deny it. The theory is looked upon by some as an almost necessary basis for clear and fruitful thinking in many different fields. Men such as Bagley and Ruediger, for example, have written books in which they make evolution the guiding principle for determining the purposes and methods of education.

The impression exists that one who believes in evolution cannot believe in religion, and that one who accepts the biblical account of the creation of man cannot believe in evolution. But the theory of evolution does not necessarily deny the existence of God or the creation of man. Even if some scientist should produce in the laboratory a living cell —a dream which has never been realized—nothing that we hold concerning God and creation would need to be changed. Abiogenesis (the origin of a living from a non-living thing) may be possible, but only because the Creator endowed non-living things with the power to give rise to life under certain circumstances. Evolution in itself is not irreligious or anti-religious. We need not fear any fact ever established by evolutionists. What we need to fear is the childish and illogical assumption to the effect that, if evolution is true, belief in God must be false.

HUMAN EVOLUTION. It would require an entire book to discuss human evolution as it should be discussed. We can only attempt to give here a few facts which will show how far scientific evidence has advanced to answer the question of human evolution.

In treating the problem of human evolution three definite phases must be considered: the evolution of the body, the evolution of the mind, and the evolution of the soul.

EVOLUTION

THE BODY. Various answers are given as to the origin of man's body. The English naturalist Darwin believed that the earliest man was a highly developed species of monkey or ape. True, the skeletal organization of the ape is strikingly similar to that of man, but on close analysis there is a vast difference in the characteristics of the skull, arms, chin, forehead, and the like. It is to be noted, however, that at most these bodily resemblances suggest that man's body and that of the ape descended from common ancestors.

In this problem the important thing to remember is that the human race has descended from a *single pair* and not from a group or tribe. Upon that fact also rests the Catholic doctrine of original sin and the redemption.

THE MIND. In recent years scientific evidence has been accumulated to show that there exists a huge chasm separating the human mind and that of the animal. This is as true of the savage as it is of the most civilized peoples. As a result, the evidence for the evolution of the human mind shows that there is little in common between man and brute creation.

If we compare uncivilized and civilized peoples *mentally,* we note that they differ in degree rather than in kind. They all possess the faculty of reasoning and the ability to form abstract ideas and judgments. They all have languages, though they differ as widely as the poles of the earth. They all have the practical and fine arts. Even their social institutions, their moral codes, their knowledge of right and wrong, and their religious ideas reflect a striking similarity in kind. Where differences do occur, they are differences of degree due in no small part to the want of education and training.

THE SOUL. The real difference between man and animal is found in the soul. By the soul we mean that spiritual principle which is substantially united with the body to form man, and because of which man possesses reason, free will, and immortality. The souls of animals do not possess these powers. They have different faculties and different capabilities. They are incapable of striving after perfection or of searching into the causes of things. They are led by instinct and not by reason. They have no spiritual nature, but, in every way, are essentially dependent on matter.

PRIMITIVE MAN. Anthropologists base their arguments for the antiquity of man on the fossil remains of man and other evidences found in the strata of the earth. Five such discoveries are most frequently discussed:

1. The Java Man, found near Trinil in Java, in 1891. It consists of a skull-pan, parts of legs, and a few fragments.

2. The Heidelberg Man, discovered in Heidelberg, Germany, in 1907. Only a lower jawbone was found.

3. The Piltdown Man, discovered in Sussex, England, in 1911. There were only fragmentary remains.

4. The Neanderthal race, of which the skeletal remains were found in 1856 near Dusseldorf, Germany. It probably includes the Rhodesian Man, discovered in a cave in Northern Rhodesia, Africa, in 1921, and the Cro-Magnon remains discovered at Dordogne, France, in 1860.

5. To this list we might also add the Pekin Man, which American anthropologists claim to be a Neanderthal.

THE AGE OF MAN. According to the present accumulated data there are some indications that man is at least 30,000 years old. This information is gathered from two sources: historical and geological. Historically it is to be observed that the various parchments, inscriptions, monuments, and other data-sources indicate that a fairly high degree of civilization prevailed back to 4200 B. C. The data, however, do not provide any evidence as to how much time elapsed from the creation of man up to 4200 B. C. On the other hand, from a geological point of view, there is some evidence from the human remains found in Europe, together with associated fauna and flora, that man lived there no less than 30,000 years ago.

What are we to do so far as the teaching authority of the Church and Bible is concerned? Neither the Church nor the Bible attempts to ascribe definite dates for the age of the human race. So long as we adhere to the *oneness* of the human race and its creation by God, we are free to base our conclusions as to the age of man on purely secular evidence.

EVOLUTION AND CATHOLIC DOCTRINE. A Catholic may believe in anything which is true. Evolution is not in itself opposed to our faith, for it was possible for God either to create every creature as it finally existed, or to give to lower forms of life the power of developing into something better. Either of the two methods would be equally wonderful, and neither one necessarily contradicts anything found in the biblical account of creation. One thing, however, you must hold: that when the proper time came, God breathed into man a spiritual and immortal soul which could not be the product of mere matter. Man did not become man until he received a man's soul.

The Church further declares that man has descended from a *single pair,* and that, as a result, man possesses essential unity. The creation of this first pair—Adam and Eve—is described in the Book of Genesis, where God is said to have formed Adam from the slime of the earth and then, after casting a deep sleep upon him, to have formed Eve from one of his ribs. It is admitted by the best Catholic scholars (see the *Catholic Encyclopedia* under "Eve," "Creation," "Evolution," and "Man") that this account of man's creation is capable of receiving different interpretations. It is in accordance with the spirit of the Church to incline toward a literal rather than an allegorical interpretation of the biblical account. But nothing that science may ever establish can conflict with what has been defined by the Church. Howsoever man came to exist, he did not become man until God by a creative act had given him that immortal soul which makes him essentially different from the lower animals.

EVOLUTION AND MATERIALISM. Some very great Catholic theologians and scientists have believed in evolution. It is quite possible that the universe has existed for millions of years, and that when God first created living things He gave them the power to develop into something still more perfect. The world was made, as we have already proved, to be man's dwelling place, and God may have taken as long as He wished to prepare it, and may have gone about preparing it in any way that seemed good to Him. We welcome any further light that can be thrown upon this problem, but we do not find that the proofs for human evolution are fully satisfactory. But it is not evolution in itself to which we object; it is that form of evolution which is known as materialistic evolution. Materialistic evolution, in its most offensive form, teaches that man is only an animal with improved habits and methods; that the animal from which man developed was merely the result of the chance union of chemical material; and that the non-living matter from which life originated was not created by God, but simply existed from an extremely remote past. Materialistic evolution denies everything that is immaterial and spiritual. It destroys free will and responsibility. It does away with any obligation of being morally good, with all hope of a future life, and with all belief in a loving Father who made us to be happy by serving Him. Materialistic evolution is one of the greatest evils of the present day. You are apt to meet it everywhere, often supported by a great display of scholarship. But no evolutionist was present millions of years ago when as he believes the processes which he attempts to describe were taking place. He arrives at his conclusions concerning these processes by reasoning upon data existing in the present. We really need not be concerned as to whether his reasoning is true or false, although, from all we know of the history of science, we feel inclined to say that it will not be accepted as true a hundred years from now. But whether true or false, his reasoning is not opposed to that further reasoning which we begin at the point where his reasoning ended. We reason that there can be no evolution without something which is transformed, and that the things so transformed could never have existed without an initial creative act on the part of God. That God created the universe and man is all we need to know. When science finally reconstructs—if it ever can so reconstruct—the entire scene in which God used His infinite creative power to make so vast a universe, there cannot possibly be any detail, any incident, at variance with what faith or reason has taught us to accept.

POINTS FOR REVIEW AND DISCUSSION

1. What is the theory of evolution? What is materialistic evolution?

2. What facts concerning evolution is a Catholic obliged to hold?

3. Imagine that an entire nation is committed to a belief in materialistic evolution, and discuss what the effect would be on (a) belief in a world to come, (b) divorce, (c) fraternal charity, (d) consideration for individual rights, (e) the attitude toward wealth and comfort, (f) the doctrine that might makes right, (g) honesty in politics, (h) the payment of a living wage, (i) the virtues required in home life.

4. The following statement from William C. Bagley, a well-known writer on education, is an example of the sweeping and unproved assertions which you will frequently meet in your later reading:

"In the human species, the organs of speech were probably evolved over hundreds of thousands of years and are passed on from generation to generation by biological heredity."

    a. Does the author provide any proof for his assertion? (Nothing significant has been omitted from the passage.)

    b. What effect would such a statement, coming from a professor who in general commands respect, have on a simple Catholic boy or girl in the freshman class of some large university? How would you advise such a young man or woman?

5. In the following passage H. G. Wells makes a greater effort to provide some proof for his theories:

"Man walks so well and runs so swiftly as to suggest a very long ancestry upon the ground. Also, he does not climb well now; he climbs with caution and hesitation. His ancestors may have been running creatures for long ages. Moreover, it is to be noted that he does not swim naturally; he has to learn to swim, and that seems to point to a long-standing separation from rivers and lakes and the sea. Almost certainly that ancestor was a smaller and slighter creature than its human descendants. Conceivably the human ancestor . . . was a running ape living chiefly on the ground, hiding among rocks rather than trees. It could still climb trees well and hold things between its great toe and its second toe (as the Japanese can to this day), but it was already coming down to the ground again from a still remoter . . . ancestry."

a. Would the fact that man could swim naturally and beautifully prove that his ancestors were fish?

b. Would the fact that man could leap from tree to tree like a squirrel prove that his ancestors were squirrels?

c. What does the author cleverly insinuate by the phrase "to this day" in the parenthesis?

d. What is your opinion of the force of the argument in the quotation?

THE NEXT LESSON

Having shown that God exists, that man was created for a certain purpose, and that man's soul is spiritual and immortal, the next question which arises is: What must man do in order to fulfill his obligations toward God? The answer to this question is that he must practice the virtue of religion. The next chapter, therefore, will be the first of several in which we study the nature of religion.

CHAPTER SIXTEEN

THE NATURE OF RELIGION

ELIGION. We must always keep in mind that God created the universe for His glory and the happiness of His creatures. Among all the creatures on earth we find that man was more favored than any other creature, for he was to enjoy a far higher happiness, and to enjoy it forever. We know that this is true, for we have just learned that man's soul is immortal; man was made by God to live forever. No other creature on earth is immortal. Hence man has been specially favored by God. This is sufficient evidence to show that God must have loved man above all other creatures on earth. There is food for thought here: God loves man more than anything else in this world. Would it not be most ungrateful if man did not acknowledge God's great love for him? Reason tells us that man *must* acknowledge this love, for to be ungrateful is to be unjust. Reason demands that we be just toward all. But to be just means that we give to everyone what belongs to him; and consequently we are bound to give to God what belongs to Him in return for what He has done for us. This giving to God of that which is due Him is but another name for religion.

There are several opinions concerning the derivation of the word 'religion.' From what word it is derived is not positively known. The most common opinion is that it is derived from the Latin word *religare,* which means 'to bind.' It expresses the fact that a bond or union exists between God and man.

MEANING OF RELIGION. The force of the word 'religion' can be easily seen if we keep in mind what we learned in the early pages of this book. We know that God created the universe and everything in it. That includes man. Now, if God had not created man, man would never have existed. Hence man, like everything else in the universe, is dependent upon God for his existence and for all that he has. This dependence of creatures upon the Creator establishes a relationship between them; it is the tie that binds the creature to his Creator; it is a relationship between a superior and an inferior. God is the superior, and His creatures who depend upon Him are the inferiors.

Of course, this relationship cannot be known except by one having reason, for it takes intelligence to understand any sort of relationship. Because man has intelligence he can understand this dependence. However, it is not enough merely to know this dependency; something ought to be done about it. For there are occasions when knowing a thing is of little value without action. Of what value would it be to us to know that our house was burning if we did not act upon that knowledge and try to put out the fire? And if we know that a friend is starving and fail to help him, it is worse for us than if we knew nothing of his condition. In other words, there are times when an act of the intellect demands an appropriate act on the part of the will. This is the case when we become aware of our relationship to God.

The intellect does its part when it knows the dependence of man upon God. But what is the duty of the will? How shall it act upon this knowledge? By subjecting itself to this knowledge; that is, by freely accepting what the intellect knows. With the intellect knowing and the will freely accepting we have a complete act of the mind. From this complete act of the mind we know the full meaning of religion. Religion, then, means the free acceptance of man's dependence on God.

PURPOSE OF RELIGION. While the relationship between God and creatures rests primarily upon dependency, yet to the intelligent mind that relationship implies something more. The relationship is not merely a subservient dependency, such as exists between a slave and his master, but rather that which exists between father and son. This point may be easily gathered from a knowledge of God's purpose and plan in creating man. In that plan one can see the goodness, kindness, and generosity of the Creator.

In the first place, God created man for His glory. By that we mean that God wanted others to honor, praise, and love Him, and He made man for that purpose. But how good and unselfish He was! He did not demand this of man without giving something in return. How well man is to be repaid! Man is to have everlasting happiness in return for giving glory to God. Such a reward is most generous coming from one who receives from us only what we are obliged to give. Hence man must recognize that God is something more than a superior; He is a good, kind, and loving superior who desires man's happiness as a parent does his child's. Man on his part desires this happiness, but is continually in doubt as to how to obtain it. Experience has taught man that, if left to himself, he makes many mistakes. In order to be certain, the wise man will appeal to God as a son to a father who he knows loves him and who wishes his happiness. So in that relationship between the creature and the Creator man will recognize the kind Father to whom he may appeal in his sorrows, trials, and misfortunes, and with whom he may commune in the perplexities of life. This communion with God by man, to obtain help to discharge his duty and to arrive at the happiness intended for him, is the purpose of religion.

SUBJECTIVE RELIGION. Religion may be looked at from different viewpoints. It may be viewed as existing in the mind of man and, as such, is called *subjective* religion. As it exists in the mind we will find that it is made up of several acts based upon the knowledge man has of his dependence upon God. Man, knowing God's plan and purpose in creating him, will recognize his dependence upon God (1) as a superior who made him; (2) as a benefactor who provides for his happiness; and (3) as a father who loves him. Man knows that these things concerning God are true. But religion is not merely an act of knowledge; it is likewise an act of submission to that knowledge. Consequently, man must submit himself to this knowledge by other acts of the mind. To God as a superior he must submit himself by an act of faith; that is, he must have the disposition to submit to God's authority in all things. To God as a provider of his happiness he must submit himself by an act of hope; that is, he must have the disposition to live in expectation of receiving what God has promised. To God as a father he must submit himself by an act of love; that is, he must have the disposition to return God's love by filial love. All these acts are virtues, and subjective religion may be summed up and defined as the habitual disposition to acknowledge God by acts of faith, hope, and charity.

OBJECTIVE RELIGION. From another viewpoint religion may be looked at objectively. To look at a thing objectively is to look at the thing in itself, as something apart from the person having it. So to consider religion objectively we look only at the beliefs man has concerning God and the customs man observes in putting those beliefs into practice. Hence objective religion may be defined as the sum of beliefs held and customs practiced by man in acknowledging his dependence on God.

POINTS FOR REVIEW AND DISCUSSION

1. From what Latin word does 'religion' come?
2. What in general is the relationship between God and man?
3. Define religion, and show that both intellect and will are included in the act of religion.

4. What is the purpose of religion?

5. What is subjective religion? How do faith, hope, and charity enter into subjective religion?

6. What is objective religion?

7. George Herbert Betts says:
"What we believe and teach about God should represent the weight of probabilities as represented by reason."

    a. Is everything we know about God only *probable,* or can you mention some things that are certain?

    b. Would it be necessary for us to impose burdens upon ourselves by living religious lives if everything we knew was only probable?

THE NEXT LESSON

There are persons who look on religion as something good for those who feel the need of it, but as unnecessary for stronger souls who can do without it. Is this true, or is religion necessary for all? The next lesson will consider this question.

CHAPTER SEVENTEEN

THE NECESSITY OF RELIGION

AN'S HAPPINESS RE-
QUIRES RELIGION.
There are some men who seem to think
that happiness can be obtained without
recourse to religion. Is it possible for us
to be happy without giving glory to God? You have often
heard the remark that man's happiness is in his own hands;
he must work out his happiness by himself. While it is to
be admitted that man's happiness is in his own hands, yet it
is not true that man can obtain that happiness unassisted.
There must be recourse to and communion with God; religion is a necessity. The proofs to support this statement
are two: (1) the proof based on God's intention in creating
man, and (2) the proof from man's nature. These proofs
follow:

1. God created man to glorify Him, and happiness was
to be the reward of man's voluntary service to God. This
we have already proved. Now to glorify God is to praise,
honor, and respect God. These acts will bring happiness.

But all these are acts of religion. Consequently we know that happiness comes from religion. That was the intention of God, and reason tells us that nothing can happen outside the knowledge and intention of God. But how do we account for people who have no religion and who yet seem to be happy? In the first place, it is very doubtful if there has ever been anybody who has not had some kind of knowledge of God and religion. All will be rewarded with happiness in so far as they live up to their sincere beliefs, whatever those beliefs may be. But it is most certain that anyone who has a true knowledge of God and of man's dependency upon Him and who still refuses to glorify Him can enjoy no true and lasting happiness. Experience proves this.

2. To have happiness is the constant and universal desire of man. Just what man must do to be happy has been debated by philosophers from times immemorial. The best answer that has ever been given by a philosopher is that offered by Aristotle, the ancient Greek philosopher. He tells us that happiness consists in living according to one's nature. Now, we know that man's nature is essentially reasonable; that is, man bases his activities on the use of his reason. Hence man must live in accordance with reason in order to be happy. But one of the chief things which reason makes known to man is his dependence upon God. Unless man acknowledges this dependence he is not living according to his nature.

JUSTICE DEMANDS RELIGION. Reason tells us many things, but perhaps there is nothing more clearly and thoroughly understood by all men than the universal truth of these statements: Everyone must receive his due; A debt must be paid; Justice must be done. These statements are based upon that clear concept of justice which is common to all right-thinking men. Now, justice demands that we give to everyone what belongs to him. To God belongs much. To God as a superior obedience, honor, and respect are due. To God as a kind, loving, and generous superior love and gratitude are due. Consequently, justice demands that love, gratitude, obedience, honor, and respect be given God by man. But these are acts of religion. Hence reason tells us that justice demands religion.

GRATITUDE DEMANDS RELIGION. One of the most important considerations in the last lesson was this: "God loves man more than anything else in this world." This truth is important for many reasons, but right here it is important because it shows why religion is a necessity. The same reasoning which tells us that justice is due, also tells us that gratitude must be given where gratitude is due. To whom belongs our gratitude more than to God? It was out of His infinite goodness that man was created. And it is upon His goodness that man depends for his happiness. Does not reason, relying upon the dictates of justice, demand that man be grateful to God for favors received? To be ungrateful is to be unjust. Perhaps no injustice is so keenly felt as that of ingratitude. It was to this that Shakespeare referred in those memorable lines: "Blow, blow, thou winter wind, thou art not so unkind as man's ingratitude" (*As You Like It,* II, 7, 174-76). If man, then, feels this so sharply, what may be said of God, who has given all to

"*What things a man shall sow . . . those also shall he reap. For he that soweth in his flesh . . . of the flesh also shall reap corruption. But he that soweth in the spirit . . . of the spirit shall reap life everlasting*" (Galatians 6:8).

man! So a refusal to acknowledge the goodness of God is the most unjust, unkind, and ungrateful act that man can perform. Reason, then, demands on the basis of gratitude that man acknowledge the goodness of God in acts of religion.

ORDER DEMANDS RELIGION. Reason also demands that order be observed; there is no happiness in disorder. Experience teaches us this truth. Wherever we find disorder we always find disaster and ruin. If man, then, wishes happiness, he must observe order. But in the common acceptation of the word, 'order' means that everything shall be in proper arrangement; that is, that everything shall observe its own proper place. When, therefore, there is a superior and an inferior, order requires that the superior should come before the inferior. Reason has shown us that man is inferior to God because he is dependent upon God. Proper arrangement or order, then, demands that man shall recognize God as superior and himself as inferior to God. Reason dictates that man shall observe that order and in his actions carry out the relationship of an inferior to God. But how shall that relationship be shown by man? As has been said before, man's nature appears chiefly in his intellect or mind. God on His part is an infinitely perfect mind. Right order, then, demands that man in his activities submit his mind to God's mind. In other words, man shall be subject to the commands of God in preference to what man thinks he would like to do. When God demands anything of man, man shall submit to these commands as coming from a mind that is superior, and consequently of much greater worth than his own. It is in religion that we learn of God's commandments. Reason, therefore, tells us of the necessity of religion, since through it we know God's commands and can conform our actions to them. In conforming to these commands we will be observing order, and consequently will gain happiness.

HONOR DEMANDS RELIGION. Again, reason tells us that, where there is superiority, honor and respect are due that superiority. Not only does reason demand that recognition be given a superior, but it demands that recognition be made with the proper degree of respect and honor; the higher the superior, the greater the honor and respect. Now, God is our highest superior, for He is the greatest of all beings. To Him, then, must be given the highest respect and honor. How shall we show the respect and honor due to God as our greatest superior? We show such respect and honor by religion, one great aim of which is to elevate the personality of God in the heart and mind of man. Reason, then, teaches us the necessity of religion in order that we may offer God the honor and respect due Him as our superior.

SOCIETY REQUIRES RELIGION. What has been said concerning the necessity of religion has been referred only to the individual. But experience and reason teach the necessity of religion for the well-being of society, which we call the state. The state, or society, is but an aggregation of men united for a common purpose. That purpose is to protect the rights of man, to promote justice, and to insure the happiness of its members. But how can the state promote justice and insure happiness if it does that which is contrary to justice? Justice, as we have already learned, demands the acknowledgment of God's superiority and of His right to love, honor, and respect. The state may not, therefore, consider itself superior to God, nor may it deny the honor and respect due to God. On the contrary, the state, which is nothing other than a group of individuals united for a common purpose, must do as a group what each of its members is obliged to do as an individual; it must honor God. Consequently religion is necessary for the state or society.

It might be well to note here that the consequences of irreligion will be the same for the state as they are for the individual man. But the consequences of irreligion to man are injustice, disorder, ruin, disaster, and unhappiness. The same may be expected, therefore, for the state. History has proved this to be true; where religion has been neglected by the members of a state, social, political, and economic decay has always followed. Religion, then, is as necessary for the state as it is for the individual.

POINTS FOR REVIEW AND DISCUSSION

1. Give Aristotle's rule for being happy.
2. Why does man's happiness require religion?
3. Why does justice demand religion?
4. Why does gratitude demand religion?
5. Why does order demand religion?
6. Why does honor demand religion?

THE NECESSITY OF RELIGION

7. Why does society require religion?

8. On which of the following would society save enormous sums of money if religion were perfectly observed: (a) prisons, (b) armaments, (c) life insurance, (d) courts, (e) fire insurance, (f) police, (g) hospitals.

THE NEXT LESSON

The next lesson will show that religion among men is not due to any of the ridiculous causes to which the enemies of religion ascribe it, but to a natural and reasonable impulse in man.

CHAPTER EIGHTEEN

THE ORIGIN OF RELIGION

IMPORTANCE OF THE SUBJECT. As we have seen, one of the popular methods used today by atheists to make their disbelief in the existence of God appear reasonable is to attack the origin of religion. Their false accusations concerning the origin of religion are many and varied. Some are openly absurd, and all of them are unreasonable; but many persons have been led astray by their arguments. It is important, then, that we know that our voluntary acceptance of God is not founded on mere sentiment, or fear, or any of the other origins to which religion is falsely attributed. It is most important to know that man worships God as the result of a dictate of reason.

RELIGION THE PRODUCT OF REASON. In this modern 'Age of Reason' everything possible has been done to eradicate from the mind of man 'superstition,' as religion has so frequently been called. Various departments of science have been called upon to explain away man's persistent belief in the existence of God, the immortality of the soul, the freedom of the will, and so forth. While many persons have become practical atheists as a result of these efforts, yet man, at heart, still believes that he is a creature of God and that he owes Him a corresponding duty. But why the persistence of this belief? If religion were but the superstition some men would have you believe, why is man not able to shake off such a childish and unfounded idea? Surely it is much easier to live a life of irresponsibility than to be weighed down by the moral demands of religion. There is only one answer to this question that reason will accept: Man cannot help being religious; he is by nature religious. This means that, no matter what or how alluring the argument may be in favor of irreligion, man necessarily adheres to religion with all its supposed inconveniences; it is a part of his nature. It is just as impossible for man to get away from religion as it is for man to stop reasoning. Both are results of forces inherent in his nature over which he has little control.

MODERN RELIGION AND REASON. If we look very closely at religion, we will find its beginnings in man's reason. It does not make any difference whether we look at man as he is today, or as he is supposed to have been in prehistoric times; his religion is and was based on the same principle. Today man rests his religion on the principle of causality. In the early lessons of this book we reasoned from effect to cause until we arrived at a First Cause, or God. From that point we reasoned that God was the Creator and we the creatures, and that, therefore, a dependency exists between Creator and creatures. Now, the recognition of this dependency in the mind of man is religion. It cannot be denied, then, that the idea of modern religion has its origin in reason.

PRIMITIVE RELIGION AND REASON. The same may be said concerning the religion of primitive man. While we are ready to admit that primitive man had not advanced in the knowledge of the world to the degree that modern man has, yet it must not be thought that primitive man was not a thinking, a reasoning man. He used the principle of causality in a manner similar to our use today. Man in primitive life reasoned from effect to cause. He saw the lightning and knew there was a cause for it. He heard the thunder and reasoned to a thunderer. He saw the forces of nature; he knew that man neither made them nor had control over them; he knew they must have had a cause, and he called that cause God.

You may hear many strange things about the religion which primitive man is supposed to have had. Whatever you may hear, remember this, that the latest and most scientific research has shown that all primitive men, wherever found, worshiped one God. The worship of several gods (polytheism) did not come into existence until evil influences had corrupted the earliest religious ideas. It was only when this came about that man began to worship one god in the thunder, another god in the lightning, and other gods in the many other forces of nature. But even here we may note two things: first, that there was usually one supreme God

If religion began in fear, it was that rational and wholesome fear which made the caveman brace his sagging walls . . while his unthinking dog lies ignorant of the need.

among these many minor gods, and secondly, that even in this worship of many gods man showed that he recognized the existence of some great force which was independent of the world. If he thought that this force was not one single force, he was mistaken; but at least he reasoned to the fact that it must exist.

FEAR. Perhaps the most prevalent false opinion of religion today is that its source is to be found in fear. This opinion tells us that primitive man did not know the real causes of the phenomena of nature, such as the tempest, lightning, thunder, death, and so forth. He thought these things were caused by an unseen power, terrible, and more potent than himself. To primitive man, therefore, this power was not only something to be feared, but something to be appeased. So man inaugurated acts of worship that were directed towards appeasing this power. These acts were the beginning of religion.

While it is to be admitted that man feared the phenomena of nature—as we still do—yet it is to be denied that religion had its *sole source* in fear. Fear is always caused by some impending evil. Evil, then, is the cause of fear; and if one can get rid of the evil, the fear will disappear. But to get rid of fear involves a process of reasoning; we must learn the cause of our fear before we can get rid of the fear. For example, sickness is an evil which we fear. We can get rid of the fear if we can get rid of the sickness. But to get rid of the sickness means to find out what is the cause of the sickness. That is why we call in a doctor. We know *when* we are sick, but the doctor is called in to find out *why* we are sick. By removing the cause, the sickness will go, and consequently the fear. But the finding of the cause of sickness and removing that cause is something that demands knowledge and the use of reason. Now, let us apply this example to the fear of the primitive man. Primitive man was afraid, and the cause of his fear was the terrifying forces of nature. In looking for the cause of these forces of nature, he attributed the cause to an unseen power. He recognized his helplessness in dealing with this unseen power, and in order that this power would not be harmful to him he tried to be friends with it by performing acts of reverence. But all this required the use of reason. Hence these acts of reverence or religion found their beginnings in the use of reason, not in fear. Fear was only the motive that caused man to think.

If it were true that fear alone causes religion, why do not animals have religion? They fear impending evils just as man does. But animals do not have reason and, therefore, cannot know the cause of anything. They cannot reason to an unseen cause, and hence they have no religion.

ANIMISM. Animism has been given by some the credit for being the basis of religion. A very superficial glance at what animism is will show this to be a false explanation of the origin of religion. Animism means the worship of ancestors. It had its origin in the belief that after death the soul takes on another life, a life more powerful and of a higher nature than the one it had when united with the body of man. Because of this belief man worshiped the souls of his ancestors as superior beings. It is evident that animism is based on the belief in the immortality of the soul. But the immortality of the soul is one of the tenets of religion. Religion, therefore, must have existed before animism, and, consequently, animism cannot be the origin of religion.

Moreover, if animism were the source of religion, how would we be able to account for the existence of religion in races of people who never had ancestor worship?

FETISHISM. Fetishism is a religious system that is based on magic. People came to the belief and practice of fetishism because they thought that man could come in contact with God only by means of a material substance. Hence they attributed to material things the powers of a god. The substance that contained the power was called a fetish. But fetishism cannot be the foundation of religion, for we find in the fetish-worshipers a pre-existing knowledge of a deity. But knowledge of, and belief in, a deity is one of the tenets of religion. Religion, then, must have existed before fetishism.

DECEPTION THEORIES. These are theories which state that the origin of religion is found in the deception of man, particularly in the legislators and priests. These theories are so illogical, so unreasonable, that no one using his reason to the slightest degree will be influenced by them.

They tell us that lawmakers wanted some means of enforcing the laws upon their subjects. With that end in view, they told their subjects that, if their laws were not obeyed, they would be punished by an unseen power who sees all and knows all—even their secret violations. This is an uneasonable and self-contradictory theory. For the subjects must have had some knowledge of, and belief in, this superior force, otherwise the lawmakers' appeal to this power would not have had any more effect upon the people than the laws themselves. Deception on the part of legislators, then, presupposes the knowledge of a deity. Hence religion existed before the deception.

The theory that religion started in the deception of priests is just as unreasonable. It has been said that in the early days there were some men who wanted the respect and honor of the rest of the people. So they deceived the people into believing that they were the representatives of superior, unseen powers. They assumed the title of priests, and it was thus that religion began to exist.

Priests may use their position for gain. They may take advantage of the simple and ignorant, but they could never have invented a God for the people. To believe that they could or did is, in itself, unreasonable. Man at all times, since the days of Adam, has been a reasoning creature. Men are frequently deceived, but not for any great length of time. Children are sometimes frightened into being good by being told: "The goblins will get you if you don't watch out." But that period in a child's life is very short. When the child comes to the use of his reason, he soon finds out that there are no goblins. No longer does childish belief in the goblins affect him. In the same manner man would have eventually reasoned to the conclusion that priests were deceivers and that no unseen power existed. Religion would then have come to an end. But after thousands of years the world has not yet come to this conclusion. The world still finds it reasonable to believe in God.

Moreover, if priests in the beginning invented a God, they really did not deceive the people, for they told them what was true. Hence religion could not have had its origin solely in the deception of priests, but had a foundation in truth.

EVIDENCES OF REASON IN RELIGION. If we examine all these theories, there is one fact that is very noticeable. No matter what the theory may be, some belief in a Supreme Being will be found at its foundation. It was such a belief that led to animism and fetishism, and the same belief was required to work out any of the 'deceptions.' These various false theories have no real facts to support them. They are imaginary explanations offered by men who are unwilling to admit the existence of God and the necessity of religion. But even if there were truth in the theory, it would still be a fact that man's reason saw how necessary it was for some Supreme Being to exist. Religion began, and religion survives today, because it appeals to the human intellect as true, reasonable, and desirable.

POINTS FOR REVIEW AND DISCUSSION

1. Show that religion, both today and in primitive times, is based upon reason.

2. Why does fear not explain religion?

3. What is animism, and why does it fail to explain the origin of religion?

4. Why does fetishism fail to explain the origin of religion?

5. Refute the deception theories of the origin of religion.

6. Read the following passage from George Herbert Betts:

"Religion was at the start the product, on the human side, of fear and apprehension. Primitive man was surrounded by forces of nature which he did not understand and which terrified him. Storms crashed about his head, floods drowned his flocks, jagged fire flashed across the heavens. Famine, pestilence, and disease took their toll of lives. Constantly he confronted the mysteries of birth and death which he could not comprehend. To him the stars moved in the sky, the sun rose and set, the seasons passed in regular procession he knew not why or how; on occasions a dark shadow seemed to be eating the sun or moon only to be driven away by much beating of drums, noise, and shouting: on all sides confusion, mystery, danger, uncertainty. The universe was too great for him.

"Then in his extremity this sorely troubled man obeyed an urge deep in his nature and reached out to Something beyond human for help. . . . He began the search for God, which is yet going on under the drive of the same need."

a. So far as you know, is this passage based on historical data or is it largely the product of the writer's imagination? Does the writer know how primitive man thought and acted?

b. Even though fear may have impelled primitive man to turn to God, is there any reason for believing that he could not and did not recognize the existence of God before he had reason to be afraid of anything?

c. This search for God, says Mr. Betts, is "yet going on under the drive of the same need." Is fear the only thing that causes men to turn to God today?

d. Do you think it makes people admire religion more to be told that religion today is merely the continuation of an attitude of mind brought about by irrational fear in ignorant and superstitious men?

7. Holy Scripture says: "The fear of the Lord is the beginning

of wisdom" (Psalm 110:10). This might appear to confirm what Mr. Betts says in the passage quoted above. Which of the two statements which follow appears to you to be more reasonable?

a. The Scripture text confirms what Mr. Betts says.

b. The text does not create any difficulty, and our reasons for saying so are as follows: (1) "Fear" does not mean a blind, irrational fear, but a proper respect for the omnipotent power of God. (2) When Scripture says that we should fear God, it takes it for granted that we first know of God's existence. (3) Scripture does not say that wisdom (in religious matters, of course) begins in fear of the forces of nature, as Mr. Betts does. It says that it begins in fear of God.

THE NEXT LESSON

If religion is as natural for man as we have said, does it not follow that man can work out by his unaided intellect a religion which satisfies all his needs? The next lesson will undertake to answer this question.

CHAPTER NINETEEN

NATURAL RELIGION

UESTIONS CONCERN-
ING NATURAL RELI-
GION. Up to this point we have
proved that God exists, that God created
man, that God created man for a definite
purpose, and that man, because of the relationship existing
between himself and God, is obliged to worship God by the
practice of religion. We already know, and we will prove
in the proper place, that man cannot worship God as he
should without accepting that religion which God Himself
has revealed to man. But what is to be said of a purely
natural religion—that is, of a religion which men develop
for themselves by the use of their reason and without any
dependence on supernatural revelation?

Does such a purely natural religion exist anywhere in the
world? Of this we cannot be entirely certain. It is true that
we have discovered tribes of men who worship a Supreme
Being in ways which seems to be the product of their own
reasoning—tribes to whom Christianity, so far as we know,
was never preached. It is also true that we find individuals

or groups of individuals working out religions of their own; little religious bodies, oftentimes with the oddest ideas, spring up constantly generation after generation. But it is impossible for us to know whether these persons have been completely unaffected by any part of the supernatural revelation which God has made. Even uncivilized tribes may have heard something about it from others. Besides, if men are sincerely endeavoring to serve God, God may make known to them, in some manner which His infinite wisdom devises, whatever supernatural truths are necessary for their salvation. For this reason we do not affirm that there ever has been, or ever could be, a religion which is purely natural. But this at least is certain, that there have been very many religions in which it is impossible for us to discover evidence of any supernatural revelation made by God—religions which, so far as we can see, are the product of man's unaided intellect, and which therefore deserve to be called natural.

We are not inquiring here whether God desires to be worshiped by a purely natural religion. We are simply taking natural religion as we find it in the world, and asking ourselves two questions concerning it: First, what ought it to be if it is to be good and satisfactory? Secondly, has it ever been what it ought to be?

QUALITIES OF A SATISFACTORY NATURAL RELIGION. A natural religion, to be good and satisfactory, should do the following things:

1. It should describe, correctly and with sufficient fullness, the nature of God.

2. It should tell us what is the true destiny of man.

3. It should make known what thoughts we should entertain and what actions we should perform if we are to worship God in the right way and achieve our destiny.

4. It should do all this with such clearness and certainty that the mind will be at rest, and that any well-intentioned person can find the answers he desires to his religious problems.

IS A SATISFACTORY NATURAL RELIGION POSSIBLE? To deny that the human intellect is able to arrive at a sufficiently correct knowledge of God would be equivalent to saying that God has made man's intellect incapable of doing the chief thing which it was made to do. But it often happens that what is theoretically possible is practically impossible. Another way of expressing this truth is to say that a thing could be done, but that it actually has not been done. It is possible for a tennis player to make every stroke so absolutely perfect that the best player in the world could never return the ball. To do this is the aim and ambition of every great player. Yet it has never been done; it is *practically* impossible. The same may be said of the effort on the part of human reason to discover the natural truths and duties of religion. History teaches us that the requirements of a perfect natural religion have never been met. Religion is most universal; there has never been a nation or tribe of people on earth where a religion of some kind did not exist. This is true of the most savage and uncivilized tribes. Yet when we examine the various religions practiced by these people, we find that where man has been left to his own reason to discover the truths and practices of religion, he has always fallen into error concerning God and his relation to God. Let us take, for example, the nation which has always been considered the most intellectual and most cultured of all nations, the Greek nation. Here we find that their religion was filled with errors. Even the man who was the most representative of the Greek nation, Aristotle, a man who as an intellectual genius ranks among the greatest of all times, made mistakes concerning man's religious duties. Great thinkers, such as Socrates and Plato, likewise fell into error. What has been said of the Greek mind can also be applied to the great minds of other nations, such as the Roman, the Hindu, or the Arabian.

When men of such superior caliber fall into religious error, what shall be said concerning men of ordinary intelligence? It is only reasonable to suppose that they too, will meet with the same difficulties. Natural religion, therefore, is inadequate to meet man's needs.

THE CAUSE OF THIS INADEQUACY. We have seen that all the efforts of man to work out a system of religion by means of his own intellect have failed. All races have believed in a Supreme Being and have realized the importance of serving that Supreme Being. But no race, without the special assistance of God, has succeeded in developing a religion free from serious limitations and even gross errors.

How can this be explained? If God made man for the one purpose of serving and glorifying Him, why did He not make it possible for man to fulfill this purpose?

We must not say that any creature of God is absolutely perfect. Only God is absolutely perfect; all His creatures

The Romans made their emperors gods . . . and "changed the truth of God into a lie, and worshipped and served the creature rather than the Creator" (Romans 1:25).

have limitations. Nevertheless, although creatures are not absolutely perfect, they are at least able to do with reasonable ease that which they were created to do. All birds, for example, could fly still more rapidly than they do, and with greater ease; but they do not suffer from inability to fly with any kind of success. How, then, can we explain the fact that man's intellect, made to know God, experiences such difficulty in doing what it was made to do?

There is only one possible explanation of this fact. Something happened to man which made it difficult for him to think clearly about God. There was some great original catastrophe. This catastrophe must have involved a sin, for only sin merits chastisement. What this sin was remains to be seen later, but for the present it explains what would otherwise be a mystery to us, and which is in fact a mystery to others.

POINTS FOR REVIEW AND DISCUSSION

1. What is natural religion?

2. What conditions must be fulfilled if a natural religion is to be complete and satisfactory?

3. Is it possible for these conditions to be fulfilled?

4. What does history tell us concerning the ability of man to arrive at a perfect natural religion?

5. Why is supernatural religion necessary?

6. George Herbert Betts says, in speaking of our concept of God:

"In all religions, from the most primitive to the most highly developed, men endow their deity with the qualities which they themselves prize and desire to possess. . . . Only a person with a strain of vindictiveness in him can believe in a God who seeks revenge. Only a person who sets a high value on the exaction of justice for wrongs committed can accept a God who demands legalistic payment for sins by suffering."

    a. Do you think this passage affirms that our idea of God is not a true idea which is formed by reasoning correctly about God's nature, but that it is a fictitious idea which is formed by attributing to God, without any necessary reason, qualities which we consider desirable? Is it true that this is how we arrive at a knowledge of the qualities of the deity?

    b. Our own faith teaches us that God demands punishment for sin. Is Mr. Betts apparently approving or condemning this idea when he speaks of "legalistic payment for sins by suffering"? What would you say in answer to this sneer?

    c. In our chapter on "The Problem of Evil" we saw that God has certain ways of acting which it is difficult fully to understand. Many Catholics would prefer not to have to admit that God has certain qualities—for example, that He is ready if necessary to condemn us to hell eternally. Yet they accept these things because they know they are true. How does this disprove the statements made by Mr. Betts?

THE NEXT LESSON

In the next lesson we will endeavor to decide what God may have done to compensate for the inability of man to develop adequate religious ideas by himself.

CHAPTER TWENTY

SUPERNATURAL RELIGION

SUPERNATURAL TRUTHS AND REVELATION. In the last chapter we saw that no natural religion has ever been completely satisfactory. Most of them have been positively bad and harmful in many respects, and even those which in the beginning were reasonably good have shown a tendency to become corrupt and sensual. But as we look around in the world we find, in addition to these natural religions, others which claim to be supernatural. A supernatural religion is one which teaches truths which were specially revealed to man by God. Is such revelation possible? Is it necessary? In how many ways can it be said to be supernatural?

DIVINE REVELATION POSSIBLE. One would not think that there was anybody so unreasonable as to deny that God can reveal truths to man if He wishes to do so. Yet there have been men who say that it is impossible. These men are called rationalists, and they tell us it is contrary to reason to think that God can manifest His thoughts to man. While these men are called rationalists, which means persons who are guided by reason, the term does not seem to fit them, for evidently they do not use reason—at least not correctly. A very small amount of reasoning, just a little 'common sense,' will show that God can reveal truths to man. When God created man He gave man the power of communicating or revealing his thoughts to his fellow man. We exercise that power in every-day speech. Would it not, then, be most unreasonable to believe that God Himself could not exercise the same power He gave to man? Moreover, the power of speech was given to man in order that men might assist each other in working out their destiny. But who is more interested in this destiny than God? To say, then, that God created man and then could not communicate assistance to him in realizing his destiny is most unreasonable. Reason proclaims the possibility of revelation.

NECESSITY OF REVELATION. In order to understand what is meant by the necessity of revelation, it will first be well to understand what is meant by necessity. A thing is necessary if some other thing cannot exist or be done without it. There are two kinds of necessity; absolute necessity and moral necessity. Absolute necessity means that a thing is so essential that the thing which depends upon it simply cannot exist without it. For example, it is absolutely necessary to have a piano in order to play a piano solo; if we do not have a piano, we cannot play the music. Moral necessity means that in theory a thing is not so essential that it would be impossible to get along without it, but that in practice we seldom if ever can do without the thing in question. For example, it is morally necessary for men to have friends and companions; absolutely speaking, men could live in solitude, but they very seldom do, for companionship is a thing demanded by their nature. Now, if we are speaking of *supernatural* religion, it is very evident that revelation is an *absolute* necessity. For supernatural religion teaches truths which man by using his reason alone could never discover. Since these truths must be known by man in order to fulfill the purpose for which he was created, it is absolutely necessary that God reveal them to him. Hence we conclude that divine revelation is absolutely necessary for supernatural religion. But what shall we say of the necessity of revelation for *natural* religion? In speaking of natural religion, we found that it was extremely difficult for man to have a perfectly clear idea of his duties toward God. We found that it is possible for man to know of his natural duties, but that as a matter of fact he never has. Consequently, we are within reason in saying that adequate, complete natural religion is *morally* impossible without divine assistance of some kind. As a matter of fact, God chose revelation as a means of instructing man in his natural duties towards Him. Hence we conclude that in order for man to have even natural religion it is morally necessary for him to have divine revelation.

KINDS OF REVELATION. There are different kinds of revelation, depending upon the quality or kind of the truth revealed and upon the manner in which the revelation

"And when Moses came down from the mount Sinai, he held the two tables of the testimony, and he knew not that his face was horned from the conversation of the Lord" *(Exodus 34:29).*

is made. Now, truth is the content, the substance of revelation. When we speak, therefore, of the kind of truth contained in revelation we use the term, 'substance' of revelation. Hence if the truths revealed are natural truths the revelation is called 'revelation natural in substance.' On the contrary, if the truths revealed are supernatural truths, then the revelation is called 'revelation supernatural in substance.' For example, if God were to make known His existence, the revelation would be natural in substance, for the existence of God is a natural truth which our unaided reason can discover. If the Blessed Trinity is revealed by God, then the revelation is supernatural in substance; no man could ever know of this truth by his reason alone.

There are two ways in which God may manifest truths. He may manifest them in a supernatural way or manner, or he may manifest them in a natural way. God is said to reveal truths supernaturally when He manifests truths to man either by word of mouth or sign. For example, at the Transfiguration of Jesus a voice was heard which said: "This is My beloved Son" (Luke 9:35), and when He was baptized, the Spirit of God descended in the form of a dove. This is not the usual way for God to communicate truths to man. It is above the natural manner; it is supernatural in manner. When we consider the revelation of the Ten Commandments to Moses we find that we have a revelation natural in substance, but supernatural in manner. The commandments (except perhaps the third) are truths that man could have known by the light of his own reason. Hence the revelation was natural in substance. But because God made known the ommandments by word of mouth the revelation was supernatural in manner.

But what is meant when we say that God reveals truths in a natural manner? Not all truths have been revealed by God by word of mouth or sign. We find that certain truths are made known through the works of creation and can easily be seen by the light of our natural reason. For example, when we look at the heavenly bodies and see their greatness and the order that reigns among them, we become aware of the power and the wisdom of God in creating them. God's works, then, reveal Him to us; they are a revelation of His attributes. Since we can come to the knowledge of these attributes by our own natural reason, this revelation is called natural revelation.

Let us summarize what we have just learned. If the truths revealed are natural the revelation will be natural in substance. If the truths revealed are supernatural the revelation will be supernatural in substance. If the revelation is made through the works of nature the revelation is natural in manner. If the revelation is made by the words of God the revelation is supernatural in manner.

POINTS FOR REVIEW AND DISCUSSION

1. What adjective do you use to describe that revelation which God makes of Himself through the works of nature and which every man receives simply because he is able to use his reason?

2. When is revelation supernatural in manner? Supernatural in substance?

3. Under what conditions is revelation absolutely necessary? Morally necessary?

4. Which of the following truths can we know by the use of reason? Which require revelation?

    a. God exists.

    b. God is a Trinity.

    c. The Mother of God was born free from original sin.

    d. God is all-powerful.

    e. God is all-knowing.

    f. Christ is present in the Blessed Sacrament.

    g. God is good and loving.

    h. Priests have the power to forgive sins.

    i. God must have had a purpose in creating man, and it is possible for man to discover what this purpose was.

5. Consider the following revelations: (a) The revelation made when a voice from heaven said: "Thou art My beloved Son" (Mark 1:11); (b) the revelation of God's power seen in the hurricane; (c) the revelation made to Ananias when God said to him: "Arise, and go into the street that is called Strait, and seek in the house of Judas, one named Saul of Tarsus. For behold he prayeth" (Acts 9:11); (d) the revelation made to the Blessed Virgin that she was to be the Mother of God; (e) the revelation made to St. Joseph when he was told to take the Child and His Mother and flee into Egypt; (f) the revelation made by Christ when He said that he who believed and was baptized would be saved.

Which of these revelations is natural in substance but supernatural in manner? Natural in substance and natural in manner? Supernatural in substance and supernatural in manner?

THE NEXT LESSON

The next lesson will take up the question: "How shall we begin to investigate the reality of a supernatural revelation?"

CHAPTER TWENTY-ONE

THE SEARCH FOR DIVINE REVELATION

**SUMMARY OF WHAT WE HAVE LEARNED.** At this point it will be helpful to review what we have already learned. We began by determining that we would use our reason, not through any disrespect for the truths taught by faith, but because it is right for us to understand the proofs for everything we know and for everything we believe. Thus using our reason, we proved that God exists, and that He must be a loving, personal God who exercises providence over the world which He made. We saw that man must be a created being, that he possesses intellect and free will, that he possessed these gifts from the beginning and is not a mere descendant of brute beasts, and that his soul is a spiritual thing which is destined to live forever. These facts made it evident to us that atheism, agnosticism, and materialism are false and unreasonable schools of thought, and that the physical and moral evils existing in the world ought not to cause a serious difficulty to any seeker after truth.

Considering, then, the fact that God is the Creator and man the creature, we saw that man has an obligation of recognizing his dependence upon God; in other words, that he must practice religion. It became evident that religion is not a mere superstitious fear, or the outcome of deceit practiced upon man by other men, but that it is a necessary result of the fact that man has a reason which can perceive his essential relationship to his Maker. But we saw also that man had never, by the use of his own reason, been able to build up a complete and satisfactory body of religious truths. (This fact made us suspect that something must have happened to affect man's intellect, since it was originally intended to serve him as a sufficient means of arriving at the knowledge necessary for his welfare.) We saw that revelation was possible. We also began to suspect that God actually did make a revelation, since man is in such need of help and God in His goodness so ready to give it. Such a divine revelation would be supernatural because it came through channels which were not natural; it might also be supernatural because it contained truths at which man's unaided reason could never have arrived.

RELIGION AND REVELATION. There are many religions in the world, and practically all of them claim to be based upon divine revelation. Catholics and Protestants claim to follow a revelation made by God through Jesus Christ. The Jews follow a revelation made by God through Moses and the prophets. Joseph Smith, founder of the Mormons, said that he had received a revelation written on golden plates and brought to him by an angel. Mohammed,

Many men have claimed to be the bearers of a message from God to man. . . . One claimant only can be true, for God does not contradict Himself. . . . There must be marks by which the true claimant can be known.

in the fourth year of his preaching, began to say that he was teaching by the command of God. It is evident that only one of these many religions can be true, for God cannot lie, and say one thing about Himself to one person and a contradictory thing to another person. We ought to determine which one is true; for if God thinks that a revelation should be made, it is evident that the revelation must be very helpful and even necessary. The problem, then, is how to distinguish true revelation from false revelation.

MARKS OF TRUE REVELATION. Who can doubt that, if God does make a revelation, He will also make it possible for men to identify it as a true revelation? Not to do this would be to frustrate His own designs. Of what benefit would it be to mankind to make a revelation if man had no means of determining whether or not it was a true revelation? Our reason tells us that a revelation made by God can be expected to have marks not found in false revelations.

What will these marks be? Before attempting to answer this question, let us note that everything which claims to be a divine revelation has been made known to us through man. It is quite evident that God could, if He so wished, appear in the heavens in some visible form and give such proofs of His omnipotent power as to convince every mind that it was indeed He who was speaking. But He has not chosen to act in this way. Every collection of true or supposedly true facts proposed to us today as a divine revelation was made known to mankind through some individual. These individuals—Jesus Christ, Moses, Mohammed, Joseph

Smith—are either God's chosen legates or not. There is no alternative.

In our search for divine revelation, therefore, the logical thing to do is to examine into the life of the individual who claims to have brought us the revelation. His life, his character, and his message should all have the stamp of God's approval upon them. It is there that we shall find the marks of divine revelation.

Jesus Christ undoubtedly deserves to be considered in the first place of all. For His life was most wonderful in its holiness, its wisdom, and its goodness. Of all who claimed to be legates, He made the most sweeping and startling statements concerning His divine mission. Millions of the wisest men of all nations and all ages have accepted His claims. No man, however prejudiced, could deny His right to have His claims examined.

But how shall we go about our examination of these claims? We must do what men do when they study any historical character; we must go to the records. The four Gospels are the original records in which the words and deeds of Jesus Christ were narrated by men of His own day. Are these documents true and dependable? Do they tell us what really happened? This is the first question to be settled. And after we have settled that, we take up two other questions: What did Jesus Christ say about Himself? and, What marks or signs did God give that Jesus Christ was speaking the truth?

In the beginning of the book we thought as philosophers, using the principles and methods of philosophical thought.

Now we must think as historians, for the task awaiting us in the next chapter is to determine whether the written records of the life of Jesus Christ are dependable historical documents.

POINTS FOR REVIEW AND DISCUSSION

1. As a matter of review, give short proof for the following:
    a. God exists.
    b. God is a personal God.
    c. God exercises providence over the world.
    d. Man is a created being with intellect and free will.
    e. Man is not descended, body and soul, from the brute beast.
    f. Man's soul is spiritual and immaterial.
    g. Atheism, agnosticism, and materialism are to be rejected.
    h. Religion is essentially natural to man.
    i. Revelation is possible.

2. Prove this proposition: If divine revelation did not have marks by which it could be identified, men would be excusable if they refuse to practice any religion.

3. Prove that, among all who claim to be divine legates, Jesus Christ is deserving of first consideration.

THE NEXT LESSON

The next lesson will open up the question of the reliability of the documents on which Christianity bases its claims.

CHAPTER TWENTY-TWO

CHARACTERISTICS OF AN HISTORICAL DOCUMENT

GENUINE REVELATION AND ITS TEST. In the preceding pages we have shown that it was not only possible for God to have revealed truths to man, but that it was very probable a revelation would be found to exist. Christianity claims that God did make a revelation and that the revelation is still in existence. However, as we have said before, many others have made that same claim. Since the revelations which various religions claim to have received from God differ essentially from one another, it is only reasonable to suppose that one of them is true and the others false. If any of these religions wish to establish the fact that God did reveal truths and that they are the custodians of His revelation, it will be necessary for them to give sufficient, reasonable proofs to support that claim. They must be able to produce an historical document establishing beyond doubt that the claims which they make concerning themselves are true.

Christianity is prepared to offer such documents. It claims to teach the one true revelation. It holds that its teachings embody the revelations that were made by God through His legate, Jesus Christ, and, in support of this claim, it offers the Gospels as documentary evidence. Our purpose, then, is to examine these documents and with an unbiased mind to proceed to test their validity. Can Christianity stand the test?

NATURE OF A DOCUMENT. Before we attempt to determine the requirements of a true and valid document, it would be well to know what a document is. According to the definition given by the dictionary, a document is an original or official paper relied upon as the basis, proof, or support of anything else. This definition here given is one that will fit any kind of a document which may be used in support of any claim. An historical document, then, will be an original or official paper that can be used to prove an historical fact. Hence the Constitution of the United States is such a document, for it is an original paper offered to prove that the people of this country have formed an agreement among themselves as to how they shall be governed. If anybody, then, should question the right of our people to govern themselves in a certain way, this document would be produced as evidence of such a right. Now, Christianity makes the claim that God at one time did make a revelation through Christ, its founder, and that it possesses historical papers to prove and support that claim. Christianity, therefore, lays claim to an historical document which offers to the world sufficient and reasonable proof that its teachings are in accordance with the revelation made by God through His ambassador, Christ.

DEPENDABLE DOCUMENTS. Not every document that is offered in support of a claim is a dependable document. In order to be a dependable document the definition requires that it must furnish 'proof that can be relied upon.' Our next point, then, is to find out what constitutes a proof. Or, in other words, when can a document be relied upon? If a document is a dependable document it should have these characteristics or qualifications: (1) it ought to be authentic, (2) entire, and (3) trustworthy. Why these characteristics are necessary will be explained in detail as the subject develops.

AUTHENTICITY. In the first place, what is meant by authenticity? Authenticity means that the document has been written by the person who is thought to have written it. No one would accept a claim as valid when supported by a document whose authorship is not genuine. We could not have any confidence in the Declaration of Independence if we were to find out that it was a forgery made by someone in 1840, and that those whose names were signed to it never saw or heard of it. There are many famous examples in history of such forged documents. If a document is to be considered dependable, we must be able to prove that he who is said to have written it actually did write it.

INTEGRITY. Integrity means that the document is entire. When is a document entire? It is entire when it has not been substantially changed. A document has been substantially changed if so much has been added or taken away that the original meaning has been lost. The reason for demanding integrity in a document is evident. If a document has been so changed by the addition or subtraction of words, sentences, or phrases that its meaning has been destroyed, it is clear that it is not a true record of the events which it describes. Surely it would not be proof of what was originally intended. A document, therefore, in order to be dependable must have integrity; it must not have been so tampered with as to have lost its original meaning.

TRUSTWORTHINESS. Furthermore, even though a document is authentic and entire, one other important quality is required if we are to place reliance on it. This is trustworthiness, which means that the author is qualified to make the statements which bear his name. Is the author truthful? Could he be deceived in what he says? Was the author in a position to know that what he says is true? These are some of the questions which we ask concerning a document, and they are grouped under the heading of trustworthiness. Certainly no man will accept a document as true unless its author can stand this test. We will not accept the testimony of any man if it can be shown that he does not possess a truthful character, or that he deliberately lied about any facts, or that he may have made mistakes in judgment concerning the facts he relates. Such a document would not be trustworthy.

Hence every document, in order to be a true and dependable historical document must have these characteristics; it must have authenticity, integrity, and trustworthiness. If any document contains in a perfect manner these three qualifications, it must be accepted as proof of the statements which it contains, and no man using his reason properly can refuse to look upon it as a true and dependable document.

POINTS FOR REVIEW AND DISCUSSION

1. Name the three qualities necessary in a true and dependable historical document.

2. If some writer living today were to write a perfectly accurate history of the Civil War and attribute it to Robert E. Lee, which quality would the document lack?

3. If an extremely bigoted and unreliable communist were to write a hostile history of capitalism, which quality would the document lack?

4. The King James version of the Bible deliberately omitted certain passages. Assuming that the translation was in other respects faultless, which quality did it lack?

THE NEXT LESSON

The next lesson will describe the four Gospels, to which we intend to apply the tests explained above for the purpose of determining whether they are dependable historical documents.

CHAPTER TWENTY-THREE

THE GOSPELS

HE MEANING OF CHRISTIANITY. In the past we have made repeated references to Christianity. Christianity is commonly used to designate the sum total of all the various religions existing today under the general title of 'Christian.' But it is evident that no document can prove that all these religions are true, since one flatly contradicts what another says. In the present discussion, then, Christianity is to be taken as referring to that body of religious believers who *actually did* receive their religion from Christ and His apostles. It is of Christianity taken in this sense that we demand proof for its assertion that it teaches truths revealed by God through His legate, Christ. In defense of its position, Christianity offers documentary evidence to be critically examined and tested. The historical evidence offered is a document called 'The Gospels.' Before we examine these evidences minutely it would be well here to give a general survey of what the Gospels are.

THE GOSPELS. From the time of the fall of Adam in

the Garden of Eden the Jews expected a Redeemer, the Messias, whose coming meant salvation to them. They looked forward with great expectation to His arrival, for not only was it to be a glorious and crowning event in the history of their nation, but a boon to all suffering humanity. After four thousand years of expectation, Christ, who claimed that He was the Messias, appeared. He lived, taught His doctrine of salvation, and died on the cross. But the Jews refused to accept the testimony of Christ and still awaited the coming of the promised Redeemer. Shortly after Christ's death the apostles announced to the whole world that the Messias had come, that the world was saved from sin by the death of the Messias on the cross, and that happiness was possible again for every man. That was good news indeed! It was from this message of good news which the apostles gave the world that the word 'gospel' takes its name. The word for 'good news' or 'good tidings' in the Latin language is *evangelium*. Those who announced the 'good tidings' in writing were therefore called 'evangelists.' In our modern English we still retain the word 'evangelist' in the original meaning of the Latin. The word 'gospel,' however, has been handed down from the old Anglo-Saxon language, from which our modern English is partly derived. In Anglo-Saxon the word for 'good' was 'god,' and the word for 'tidings,' 'news,' or 'message' was 'spell.' Hence we have the modern word 'gospel' (godspell), meaning 'good tidings.'

THE NUMBER OF GOSPELS. It must be remembered that the apostles and disciples preached by word of mouth

first, and that later some of them wrote down what they preached. Even before they wrote anything their preachings were called the Gospel, for they contained 'good news' for the world. It was the message of the Christ to the world. Jesus, Himself, said: "Preach the gospel to every creature" (Mark 16:15). At this time we find the word 'gospel' used only in the singular. But when the evangelists wrote down the good news of the Messias' arrival and message, the word 'gospel' was used in the plural. But it must not be thought that, since 'gospel' was used in the plural, there were several different messages of the Messias. There is only one message or Gospel, just as there is only one doctrine of salvation. That was perfectly understood in the very earliest days of the Church. The number of the Gospels refers to the number of the writers and not to the number of messages.

THE WRITERS OF THE GOSPELS. There were four who wrote about Christ's life and the truths He taught: St. Matthew, St. Mark, St. Luke, and St. John. When we speak of any one of the Gospels we always refer to it as the Gospel *according* to St. Matthew, or St. Mark, or St. Luke, or St. John. It was not St. Matthew's message, but the message of the Messias. The evangelists were not the authors of the Gospel, but merely the historians of the Gospel.

The order of the Gospels is usually taken from the order of the time in which they were written. St. Matthew wrote the first Gospel, St. Mark the second, St. Luke the third, and St. John the fourth. All the Gospels were written before the close of the first century, and the first three were written during the lives of many who were eyewitnesses of events in the life of Christ and the hearers of His doctrine.

THE SYNOPTIC GOSPELS.

As we have said previously, there is but one doctrine of salvation and consequently only one Gospel. We find that the evangelists, in writing the historical account of this Gospel, included substantially the same material. In all four Gospels Christ is the central figure. His claims to divinity, the miracles He wrought in support of those claims, and His death for the redemption of mankind are described in great detail. One Gospel, however, may mention incidents omitted in another. The first three Gospels, however, are strikingly similar to one another. In the early days of Christianity it was customary to place these three Gospels in columns side by side, and they were called the Synoptic Gospels because they have a common point of view. The Gospel according to St. John, composed at a much later date, was written from a viewpoint quite different from that of the other three. What he wrote, because it contains but little of the subject matter of the other three, has always been considered as supplementary to the Synoptic Gospels. But St. John is in perfect agreement with the other evangelists in regard to the outstanding characteristics of Christ. All represent Him as truly divine.

THE LANGUAGE OF THE GOSPELS.

The language used among the Jews was the Hebrew. But the Hebrew language had many dialects. The dialect used at the time of the apostles was called Aramaic, and this was the language used by Christ. Although three of the evangelists were Jews, only one of the Gospels was written originally in the Aramaic. St. Matthew, who was called the Apostle of the Jews, wrote his Gospel in Aramaic because he intended it for the Jewish people. A few years after it was written it was translated into Greek. The other evangelists wrote for the Gentiles and used the Greek language. None of the original Gospels is in existence today. Copies, however, were made in different languages during the lives of the evangelists. Old copies are still in existence and are used today as texts of Christ's teaching. That these texts are genuine historical documents will be proved in the following lessons.

POINTS FOR REVIEW AND DISCUSSION

1. What does the word 'gospel' mean?

2. Was there a Gospel before the Gospel existed in written form?

3. Name the four Gospel writers.

4. Why do we speak of the Gospel 'according to' St. Matthew and not the Gospel 'of' St. Matthew?

5. What do we mean by the Synoptic Gospels?

6. In what languages were the Gospels written?

THE NEXT LESSON

The next lesson will apply to the Gospels the first test, that for authenticity.

CHAPTER TWENTY-FOUR

THE AUTHENTICITY OF THE GOSPELS

**AITH AND REASON.**
Christianity has appealed to the world to
follow its teachings, to adhere to its faith.
It claims that its teachings are based upon
truths revealed by God through His le-
gate, Jesus Christ. In support of this claim it offers the four
Gospels as historical documentary evidence. Now, that claim
is only just as good as the evidence upon which it rests. Let
us examine this evidence and find out if all the characteristics of a true historical document are present. If we find
that this document conforms to the demands of an historical document, we are bound to accept the truth of this
claim. Moreover, if that claim is proved to be valid, then,
again, we are bound to accept the teachings of Christianity
and base our lives upon its truths. To believe in Christianity,
then, will not be a matter of blind, unreasonable faith, but
it will be one of *reasonable* faith, a faith in harmony with
the nature of man. On the contrary, if an investigation of
this evidence shows a false claim on the part of Christianity,

then Christianity is to be branded as false, deceptive, and unworthy of acceptance.

MARKS OF AUTHENTICITY. It must be remembered that, in order to have a true historical document, three conditions must be fulfilled: the document must be authentic, entire, and trustworthy. In this lesson we shall confine ourselves to one condition only: authenticity.

A document is authentic when it can be established beyond reasonable doubt that it was written by the person who is credited with having written it. But how are we to establish a fact of that kind? How are we to know in our case whether Saints Matthew, Mark, Luke, and John were the writers of the Gospels? Are the Gospels actually their work? Our only method is to examine the Gospels thoroughly and see if there are any marks or signs to indicate their authenticity. Such marks are of two kinds: external and internal. External marks are signs outside the document itself, such as the testimony of people living at the time; while the internal marks are signs right in the document, such as references to laws and customs of the people living at the time the document was supposed to have been written. Now the question is: Have the Gospels such external and internal marks as guarantee beyond reasonable doubt their authenticity?

EXTERNAL MARKS. Perhaps no document ever written can furnish such external marks of authenticity as those of the Gospels. Their authenticity was a fact accepted without qualification by (1) Christian writers, all of whom were members of the newly established Church, and (2) heretical writers who were the enemies of Christianity.

1. In the infant days of Christianity we find men of great learning—ecclesiastical writers, some even the immediate disciples of the writers of the Gospels—not only quoting passages from the Gospels, but even testifying to their authenticity. Not one dissenting voice concerning the authenticity of the Gospels can be found among them. They knew the Gospels, and some knew the writers of the Gospels; yet these men were willing to lay down their lives for the truths contained in the Gospels, and in many cases actually did do so. Is it reasonable to think that a man—particularly a learned man, one who has the opportunity to find out the truth of things—would be willing to sacrifice even life itself for something that might be false? *Learned* men do not act in that manner. These men lived at a time when it was possible to obtain first-hand information concerning the writers and their writings. Would it not be most unreasonable, then, to reject their testimony to the effect that the Gospels were genuine?

While it is not possible here to quote all the authorities of this period, a few examples will suffice to demonstrate this point. For very early evidence of the authenticity of the Gospels let us refer to St. Papias, the bishop of Hierapolis. He was very probably a disciple of St. John, and in his writings refers to the Gospels of St. Matthew and St. Mark. Then there was the testimony of St. Polycarp, another disciple of St. John, who defends the genuineness of the Gospels. And there was St. Ignatius, called 'The Martyr,' who was appointed bishop of Antioch by either St. Peter or St. John, and who sealed his testimony to the genuineness of the Gospels with his life's blood as early as the year A. D. 107. St. Justin followed his example in martyrdom about the year A. D. 165. Surely the testimony of these noted saints and many others cannot be passed over lightly.

2. Perhaps the strongest testimony comes from the heretical writers of the early days of Christianity. While these men frequently attacked the doctrines of Christianity, they never at any time denied the authenticity of the Gospels. Every one of the early centuries contributed some powerful leader to the anti-Christian forces. There was Celsus in the second century, Porphyrius in the third, and Julian the Apostate in the fourth. Yet, while all these men were the bitterest enemies of Christ and His teachings, they never attempted to denounce the Gospels as forgeries. It would have been much easier to destroy Christianity by attacking its foundations, the Gospels, than by attacking some particular doctrine contained in the Gospels. And these men, although heretics and enemies of Christianity, were learned men and would have taken advantage of any weakness they found in the foundations. But so well known and established was the genuineness of the Gospels at this early date that they realized that such a method of procedure would have been useless. The attack of the enemies of Christianity upon the *contents* of the Gospels is sufficient proof that the Gospels themselves were genuine and authentic.

INTERNAL MARKS. One of the surest and quickest methods of detecting a forgery in an historical document is

"There are some that would pervert the Gospel of Christ.
. . . But though we, or an angel from heaven, preach another Gospel to you besides that which we have preached
to you, let him be anathema" (Galatians 1:7-8).

to make a comparison of the language, customs, laws, habits, and so forth, of the people described in the document with those known from reliable sources to be in vogue at the time described. For example, if we wish to determine the authenticity of the Constitution of the United States of America, we examine the language in which the document was written. If we find that the language is different from that used in this country in the eighteenth century, we know that the Constitution was not written by anyone living in the eighteenth century. Or, if any reference were made in that document to the use of the telephone or automobile, we would know that the Constitution was not genuine or that it was not the original Constitution, for there were no telephones or automobiles when the Constitution was adopted. In the Gospels we find no such discrepancies. The men who wrote the Gospels were very familiar and conversant with the language, customs, habits, laws, and manners of the people whom they describe. In fact, historians—even those who are enemies of Christianity—tell us that the writers must have lived at the time when they are said to have written these Gospels, since no one could possibly describe the people and their customs more accurately than the evangelists. For that reason both ancient and modern historians agree that the Gospels must have been written at the time and by the writers to whom they are ascribed.

In conclusion, since the external and internal marks of authenticity are present, we must admit Christianity's claim that the Gospels are authentic; that is, that they were written by Saints Matthew, Mark, Luke, and John. Moreover, this has been the claim of Christianity from its very earliest date, and Christianity is entitled to make this claim until the contrary has been proved. No successful attempt has ever been made to dispossess Christianity of this claim.

POINTS FOR REVIEW AND DISCUSSION

1. What is meant by authenticity?

2. What difference does it make whether or not a document is authentic? For example, what difference does it make whether the first Gospel was written by St. Matthew, or by Pontius Pilate or King Herod?

3. Prove that the four Gospels have the external marks of authenticity.

4. Prove that the four Gospels have the internal marks of authenticity.

5. Debate this proposition: "The members of this class have at this moment more evidence for the fact that the first Gospel was written by St. Matthew than they have for the fact that Washington's Farewell Address was written by Washington."

6. George Herbert Betts speaking of the four evangelists, says: "Both Matthew and Luke drew upon the earlier writing of Mark for a part of their materials, and it is evident that all three had access to some still earlier manuscript or notes which have been lost. The writer of the Gospel called John is not known . . . It is thought that he belongs to a somewhat later period than do Mark, Matthew and Luke."

a. In what sense would it be wrong for one writer to "draw upon" another?

b. Under what conditions might we admit that the Synoptic Gospels all "drew upon" some earlier source?

c. St. John, in the closing chapter of his Gospel, describes the scene when St. Peter, turning about, saw the disciple who had leaned on Jesus' breast at supper; and St. John then goes on to say: "This is that disciple who giveth testimony of these things and hath written these things; and we know that his testimony is true" (John 21:24). If, then, St. John belonged to 'a later period,' was he or was he not an outright liar?

THE NEXT LESSON

The next lesson will apply to the Gospels the second test, that of integrity.

CHAPTER TWENTY-FIVE

THE INTEGRITY OF THE GOSPELS

HISTORICAL INTEGRITY

In the last chapter we proved that the documentary evidence offered by Christianity in support of its claim to a divine revelation had one point in its favor: authenticity. Christianity was able to prove that the Gospels were written by those whose names they bore. However, that does not completely satisfy the requirements of an historical document; our investigation must go farther. We wish to know whether the Gospels as we have them today are substantially the same as when the evangelists wrote them. In other words, are the Gospels entire? Have they been changed or altered since they left the hands of the writers? Have changes been made to such an extent that they no longer retain their original meaning? These are the questions that must be answered now.

In order to prove the integrity of the Gospels, Christianity offers the following argument, an argument that certainly must appeal to any reasonable man. Christianity argues that, if these Gospels have been altered substantially, the changes were made (1) either before any translations of the Gospels were made, (2) or while the translations were being made, or (3) after the translations were made. But Christianity can offer reasonable proofs that no substantial changes have been made during any of these periods. Hence Christianity's claim to the integrity of the Gospels must be admitted. Let us now proceed to look into each one of these periods and see if any alterations were made in the Gospels.

BEFORE THE TRANSLATIONS. Christianity has been able to trace back the translations of the Gospels to the first quarter of the second century. If any changes were made before the translations, they must have been made during the time of the apostles or their immediate disciples. Now, it is most improbable that this could have happened because of the attitude of the apostles and the people. Certainly the apostles and the disciples of Christ would not have tolerated any changes in the Gospels. They preached and defended with their lives the teachings of Christ, and it is most unreasonable to suppose that they would have permitted changes to creep in. So careful were they in keeping the Gospels free from changes that we find St. Paul instructing the people to beware of false gospels. "If anyone preach to you a gospel besides that which you have received, let him be anathema" (Galatians 1:9). On several occasions false gospels were circulated among the people, but they were immediately suppressed by the Church.

Nor would the early Christians have permitted any changes. It must be remembered that the Gospels were read publicly in the churches at that time. The people knew these Gospels well, and they loved and respected them so much that many of them shed their blood in defense of them. Would it be reasonable to think, then, that they would have permitted any changes to take place in such important documents?

Now, while it is most probable that neither the apostles nor their disciples nor the people would have permitted substantial changes in the Gospels, Christianity offers a still stronger proof from the writings of the Fathers of the Church. The Fathers of the Church were learned men who explained and commented upon the doctrines contained in the Gospels. They quoted passage after passage from them. In fact, their quotations are so numerous that it would be an easy task to reconstruct the four Gospels, almost in their entirety, from the quotations found in the Fathers. Now, the point to be noted is that these passages quoted from the Gospels by the Fathers of the Church are substantially the same as the passages which we read in the Bible today. There is only one conclusion to be drawn from this evidence: the Gospels as we have them today are substantially the same as the original Gospels.

IN THE TRANSLATIONS. The original manuscripts of the four Gospels are not in existence today. This fact can be easily explained. The Gospels were written by the evangelists not so much with the intention of handing down the teachings of Christ to a distant posterity, but more to satisfy the needs and demands of that time. Men well instructed in the teachings of Christ were few in comparison with the needs of Christianity. Consequently the Gospels were written by the evangelists so that the people might not be led into error concerning the doctrines of Christ. Accordingly, the Gospels were read in the churches publicly in the absence of the apostles and their disciples. It is not difficult to see, then, how these documents would not endure for any length of time because of such frequent usage. Hence copies were made to meet the needs of Christianity, and translations were also made for the sake of those who did not understand Greek or Aramaic.

There are three ancient translations still in existence, the oldest of which are the old Latin, which in St. Jerome's revision is known to us today as the Vulgate, and the Syriac. Both of these translations date back to the middle of the second century. Another translation, the Coptic, dates back to the end of the second or the beginning of the third century. Now, when these translations were made, did any substantial changes creep in? In answer to this we find, on comparing the different translations with one another, that there is no substantial difference in their texts; they all contain the same doctrines and truths, each translation expressing the same contents with the same meaning. So noticeable is this agreement that there is only one conclusion to make: they drew their material from the same source. This means that they must have used the same original texts in making their translations. It is true that we frequently find different readings, called variants; but these differences are insignificant, and no really substantial changes can be discovered. The essential message of all the translations is the same.

In comparing the Gospels, then, as we have them today with the ancient translations, we find that our present Gospels are still intact; that is, they still possess the original meaning as it was expressed in the ancient translations. Since the ancient translations were made without change from original manuscripts, it follows that the Gospels of today are entire.

AFTER THE TRANSLATIONS. This is the simplest point for Christianity to prove. Since the second and third centuries the Gospels have been copied and translated more times than any other written document in existence. If we but take a copy of the Gospels as they are printed today, it is a very easy task to find out whether or not they have been substantially changed. On examining and comparing the various editions of the Gospels existing today with the ancient translations of the second and third centuries, we find that the Gospels offered by the Catholic Church are the only ones that have not been substantially changed. Christianity has offered sufficient evidence that the original Gospels are still in existence, with their content and meaning substantially unchanged. Hence the Gospels are entire.

POINTS FOR REVIEW AND DISCUSSION

1. What is meant by integrity?

2. Prove that no substantial changes were made in the Gospels before they were translated into other languages.

3. Prove that no substantial changes were made in the Gospels when they were being translated into other languages.

4. Prove that no substantial changes were made in the Gospels now used in the Catholic Church after the translations were made.

5. We have spoken of 'substantial' changes. Which of the following facts recorded in the Gospels could not have been omitted without bringing about a substantial change:

    a. Pontius Pilate's wife had a dream about Jesus.

    b. Jesus claimed to be the Son of God.

    c. St. Peter's mother-in-law was cured of a fever.

    d. It was about the third hour when Jesus was crucified.

    e. Jesus rose from the dead on the third day.

    f. St. Mary Magdalen went to the sepulcher on Easter morning.

    g. Jesus made St. Peter the head of His Church.

THE NEXT LESSON

The final test of a dependable historical document, that of trustworthiness, will be applied to the Gospels in the next lesson.

CHAPTER TWENTY-SIX

THE TRUSTWORTHINESS OF THE GOSPELS

HIRD REQUIREMENT OF A DOCUMENT. In the chapter on the characteristics of an historical document we found that, before any document can be accepted as a true historical document, three conditions must be fulfilled: it must be authentic, entire, and trustworthy. So far the Gospels have been able to meet two of these requirements: authenticity and integrity. The third requirement is to be met in this chapter.

We have established the fact that the Gospels were written by Saints Matthew, Mark, Luke, and John and that these Gospels as they exist today have the same contents as the original manuscripts. Now the questioning goes still further. We wish to know whether the writers told the truth. Were they sincere in what they wrote? Or, even if they were sincere, was it possible that they could have been mistaken? There are many questions of this kind that might be asked, but they can all be summarized in these two questions: (1)

Were the writers *deceivers?* (2) Were the writers *deceived?* If Christianity can prove that both of these questions can be answered in the negative, then Christianity's document, the Gospels, must be accepted as trustworthy.

THE WRITERS WERE NOT DECEIVERS. When we ask the question: "Were the writers deceivers?" we really mean: "Did the writers wish and intend to deceive the world by their works?" To anyone who is at all familiar with the lives, characters, and ambitions of these four evangelists the question is hardly necessary. To those who are not, the question is easily answered by facts that will appeal readily to an unprejudiced mind.

1. In the first place, it is not reasonable to suppose that the evangelists desired to deceive. If a man wishes to deceive anyone else, he certainly must have some end in view that would be to his advantage. But what advantage was there for the writers in deception? Death! All except St. John died martyrs. Surely there was no advantage in that. And they died defending what they wrote. That is why they are called martyrs, for the word 'martyr' comes from the Greek and means 'a witness.' The writers, then, died as witnesses to the truth of what they wrote. If what they wrote were not true and they wished to deceive, would they have died martyrs in witness to and in defense of lies? Reasonable men do not act in that manner.

But perhaps they did not anticipate death as a reward of their works. Perhaps they intended to raise themselves in the estimation of the people and thereby gain the praise and rewards of heroes. Such an argument is easily settled.

A glance through their writings will show that they pictured themselves as anything but heroes. A man who wishes to be thought a hero does not reveal his cowardice and weaknesses; and yet in many places in the Gospels we find the writers most mercilessly exposing their unheroic traits of character. If the writers wished to be heroes, then, how unreasonable was their method of procedure!

2. But were the writers reasonable men? Were they intelligent beings? That question can hardly be asked. Witness the effect of their preaching upon the world! Before the death of the last apostle the Gospel was preached in every country in the world as it was known at that time. The commandment of Christ to His apostles to "teach all nations" had been fulfilled. Certainly that work could not have been accomplished except by intelligent men, and much of it was done by the writers of the four Gospels.

3. But even had they wished to deceive the world, they could not have done it. Being intelligent men, they surely would have realized that. It must be remembered that what they wrote about was witnessed by thousands of others. Moreover, they preached these same things publicly to those who witnessed them. Would reasonable, intelligent men think they could deceive people who saw and heard the things they wrote about?

4. Again, while we must admit that they were intelligent men, yet their intelligence could not have led them to the extent of inventing a character such as that of Christ, their Master. This is perhaps the strongest argument of all for the fact that the writers were not deceivers. The character

of Christ, as we shall learn a little later, was of such a noble, majestic, and superhuman type that the combined efforts of the reasoning mind of an Aristotle, the inventive genius of an Edison or a Marconi, and the dramatic ability of a Shakespeare could never have fashioned it, much less the minds of the evangelists, who had been called from the humblest ranks of life.

THE WRITERS WERE NOT DECEIVED. Surely the arguments given above will satisfy any inquiring mind as to the sincerity of the evangelists. Even a cursory reading of a few chapters of any one of the Gospels would indicate the simplicity of purpose with which they wrote. Yet is it not possible that the writers could have been mistaken in what they believed? Could it not have happened that they were deceived in the facts they related and believed to be true? When we read through the Gospels we notice that everything written concerns a central figure, that of Christ. Who He was will be taken up later. It is sufficient here to know that the entire contents of the Gospels are concerned with the works and teachings of Christ. If, then, the writers were deceived, it must have been by two things: (1) the teachings of Christ or (2) the works of Christ.

1. The evangelists would have been deceived by the teachings of Christ if, for example, they had believed on Christ's authority that baptism is necessary when as a matter of fact it was not necessary. But to hold that the evangelists were deceived in this way would be to implicate Christ in the deception, for what they wrote they received from Christ. Christ, then, must have deceived them. The fact that Christ

was not a deceiver is a subject that shall receive due consideration later on. Postulating, then, the fact that Christ did not and could not deceive anyone, we find that the writers were not deceived by the teachings of Christ.

2. Nor were the writers deceived by the works of Christ. If they were deceived, so were all the apostles, and so were all those who witnessed Christ's works, even his enemies. Now, it is not reasonable to suppose that everybody who saw Christ's works was deceived. They were works that were performed publicly before the eyes of thousands. They were extraordinary works, attracting the attention of all. Even the enemies of Christ admitted the marvelous works of Christ, but claimed that He performed them by the power of Satan and not by the power of God. How could anyone reasonably think, then, that the writers were deceived? Each of the evangelists could have applied to himself what St. John said at the end of his Gospel: "This is that disciple who giveth testimony of these things, and hath written these things; and we know that his testimony is true" (John 21:24).

It is true that only St. Matthew and St. John were eye-witnesses of the events in the life of Christ. But St. Mark wrote his Gospel under the guidance of St. Peter, and St. Luke wrote his under the guidance of St. Paul. In a certain sense we might almost say that their Gospels were the work of St. Peter and St. Paul, just as we attribute to any writer a work which was written by a confidential secretary under his direction. No one has ever questioned the fact that St. Mark and St. Luke are as trustworthy as St. Matthew and

St. John. And even if the authority of St. Mark and St. Luke were completely rejected, we would still have two writers who were eyewitnesses of the events which they relate.

POINTS FOR REVIEW AND DISCUSSION

1. Give four arguments to prove that the evangelists were not deceivers.

2. Show that the evangelists were not deceived.

3. Some years ago the archbishop of one of our large cities was to lay the cornerstone of a new church. The details of the ceremony and the names of those who were to participate were given to the press in advance. On the day appointed for the laying of the cornerstone the archbishop fell ill and the ceremony was postponed. The next morning, however, the papers published accounts of the ceremony as if it had actually taken place.

Using not only the material in this lesson, but that also in previous lessons, compare the Gospel account of the death of Christ on the cross with the newspaper account of the laying of the cornerstone. Which is more dependable, and why?

THE NEXT LESSON

Having now established the fact that we can rely upon the Gospels, our next task is to determine what the Gospels tell us concerning their central figure, Christ.

CHAPTER TWENTY-SEVEN

JESUS CHRIST WAS TRULY MAN

ESUS CHRIST TRULY LIVED. To one who accepts the Gospels as historical documents there can be no doubt whatsoever that Jesus Christ truly existed. He is the central figure in every Gospel from the beginning to the end. At every moment His commanding personality is kept before our eyes. The entire purpose of all four Gospels is to tell what He did and what He said. And Jesus is placed before us, not as an imaginary character, but as a man who actually existed.

This testimony of the evangelists is confirmed by that of Jewish and pagan historians. Flavius Josephus, a Jewish historian who died in the year A. D. 93, says: "There lived about this time Jesus, a wise man, if it be right to call him a man, for he was a doer of wonderful deeds." To this non-Christian testimony may be added that of Suetonius, who lived from A. D. 81 to 138, of Tacitus, who wrote his Annals in A. D. 115, and of Pliny, who wrote in A. D. 111. All these bear witness to the fact that Christ actually lived, and that He lived at the time indicated by the evangelists.

DOUBTS CONCERNING CHRIST. But there are men living today who deny that Christ ever existed. According to them, He is an imaginary figure representing the strivings and yearnings of the human race for perfection. He is like the creation of some poet—like Sir Galahad, for example, in the *Idylls of the King*.

It is difficult for us to understand how any human mind could ever accept any theory such as this; but when men are more interested in building up a theory than they are in searching for the truth in an honest and scientific manner, it is wonderful to what lengths they can go. Can we believe that the four evangelists, writing at different times and in parts of the world far distant from one another, painted a purely imaginary figure in almost identical language? Can we believe that they would adore as God this creation of their own imaginations, that they would urge all mankind to adore this same creation, and that they would lay down their lives for its sake? And even if we were to admit that they *might have done* all this, what evidence is there for the fact that they *did* do it?

The theory is ridiculous, but the very fact that it exists shows how important it is to study the Gospels carefully for the purpose of discovering just what they say about Christ. In this chapter we will search for evidence showing that Christ was truly a man.

CHRIST HAD A HUMAN NATURE. We find, then, that the Gospels represent Christ as possessing a human

"*And He went down with them, and came to Nazareth, and was subject to them. . . . And Jesus advanced in wisdom, and age, and grace with God and men*" (Luke 2:51-52).

nature similar to that of any one of us. Let us gather together the evidence for this fact, so that no doubt concerning it may ever remain.

1. Christ was born, was wrapped in swaddling clothes, and was laid in a manger. The beautiful story of His birth is so familiar to every Christian that there is no need to reproduce it here.

2. Christ remained a helpless infant for some time just as all children do. When His parents took Him to be presented in the Temple, the holy old man Simeon "took Him into his arms" (Luke 2:28). Later St. Joseph "took the Child and His Mother" and fled into Egypt to escape the plot of the wicked Herod.

3. Christ grew up like any other child would grow. He was subject to His parents, and "advanced in wisdom and age and grace with God and men" (Luke 2:51-52).

4. He suffered from hunger as other men do. "And when He had fasted forty days and forty nights, afterwards He was hungry" (Matthew 4:2). After His resurrection, in order to prove to His apostles that it was truly Himself, He said to them: "Come and dine" (John 21:12).

5. He was also subject to thirst as other men are: for when He was dying on the cross He said: "I thirst" (John 19:28).

6. He felt fatigue and weariness as we do. "Now Jacob's well was there. Jesus, therefore, being wearied with His journey, sat thus on the well" (John 4:6).

7. He was even subject to temptation, not in the sense that He trifled with it as we may sometimes do, but in the

sense that He actually felt difficulties. St. Matthew (4:1) tells us how He was tempted by the devil. In His agony in the Garden He revealed how keenly He felt His sufferings when He said: "My Father, if it be possible, let this chalice pass from Me" (Matthew 26:39). Dying on the cross, He cried out: "My God, My God, why hast Thou forsaken Me?" (Matthew 27:46).

8. He had human feelings as we all have. He felt so keenly the woes that were to fall upon Jerusalem that He wept: "And when He drew near, seeing the city, He wept over it" (Luke 19:41). Again He wept before the tomb of Lazarus (John 11:35), so that the Jews exclaimed: "Behold how He loved him!" (John 11:36). He loved many others in addition to Lazarus. He loved Martha and Mary (John 11:5), He loved the young man who came to inquire how he might be perfect (Mark 10:21), he loved St. John with a special love (John 13:23), and His love was faithful and constant: "Having loved His own who were in the world, He loved them unto the end" (John 13:1).

9. Finally, after living like other men, Jesus died like other men: "And Jesus, again crying with a loud voice, yielded up the ghost" (Matthew 27:50).

How can we doubt that Christ possessed a true human nature? He was undoubtedly a man. St. Paul is justified when he says: "For we have not a high priest who cannot have compassion on our infirmities, but one tempted in all things like as we are, without sin" (Hebrews 4:15). He was a man in the fullest sense of the word. Anyone who denies that He actually existed and that He was a real human being is deliberately closing his eyes to an overwhelming mass of evidence.

POINTS FOR REVIEW AND DISCUSSION

1. Quote passages from the Gospels showing that Christ:
   a. Was born as a helpless infant.
   b. Grew as other children do.
   c. Suffered hunger.
   d. Suffered thirst.
   e. Suffered weariness.
   f. Suffered temptation.
   g. Wept.
   h. Loved His friends.
   i. Died.

2. Tell the class of any other Scripture passages showing the true human nature of Christ.

3. H. G. Wells makes an issue of the fact that Roman literature contains no extended treatment of the life of Christ. How would you answer this objection, if it is one?

THE NEXT LESSON

Christ was human. But was He a mere human being with no special commission from God? This will be discussed in the next lesson.

CHAPTER TWENTY-EIGHT

CHRIST'S CLAIM TO MESSIAHSHIP

HRIST CLAIMED TO BE GOD'S LEGATE. When God revealed His will to Moses, everyone was obliged to accept the revelation thus made, for God had appointed Moses His legate. In a similar manner we would be obliged to accept the teachings of Jesus Christ, even though He were not God, if God had made Him His legate and authorized Him to teach in His name. Did Jesus Christ claim to be this legate? Did He claim to be the Messias so long expected by the Jewish people?

The passages in the Gospels which show that Christ claimed to be sent by God are so numerous that we can select only a few of them. When eating the Last Supper with His apostles, Jesus prayed to the Father, saying: "As Thou hast sent Me into the world, I also have sent them into the world" (John 17:18). Again He said: "I seek not My own will, but the will of Him that sent Me" (John 5:30). You remember also the occasion when Christ con-

versed with the woman at Abraham's well. In the account
of this event we read these words: "The woman saith to
Him: 'I know that the Messias cometh (who is called
Christ); therefore, when He is come, He will tell us all
things.' Jesus saith to her: 'I am He, who am speaking with
thee'" (John 4:25-26).

But have we nothing better than these claims made in
private to one or to a few individuals? Yes, we have many
instances in which Christ made such claims publicly; and
perhaps the most impressive is the one narrated by St. Luke.
Jesus had gone into the synagogue to teach, and Scripture
tells us in the following words what happened:

And the book of Isaias the prophet was delivered unto Him. And
as He unfolded the book, He found the place where it was written:
"The Spirit of the Lord is upon Me. Wherefore He hath appointed
Me to preach the Gospel to the poor, He hath sent Me to heal the
contrite of heart; to preach deliverance to the captives, and sight
to the blind; to set at liberty them that are bruised, to preach the
acceptable year of the Lord, and the day of reward." And when
He had folded the book, He restored it to the minister, and sat
down. And the eyes of all in the synagogue were fixed on Him.
And He began to say to them: "This day is fulfilled this scripture
in your ears" (Luke 4:17-21).

ALL KNEW OF CHRIST'S CLAIM. After Jesus had
raised from the dead the son of the widow of Naim, all the
people began to speak of Him as a great prophet. "And
this rumor of Him went forth throughout all Judea, and
throughout all the country round about" (Luke 7:17).
Nathaniel, who came to see Jesus by night, said to Him:
"Rabbi, we know that Thou art come a teacher from God

for no man can do these signs which Thou dost, unless God be with Him" (John 3:2). Finally, when Jesus after His resurrection met the two disciples on the way to Emmaus, they told Him what had happened to "Jesus of Nazareth, who was a prophet, mighty in work and word before God and all the people" (Luke 24:19). It is evident, then, that Christ claimed to be God's legate and that the people in general knew that He made this claim.

THE CLAIM TO SUPREME TEACHING POWER.

If we compare Christ with Moses or any other one of the prophets, we observe that He taught with far greater authority and finality. "And they were astonished at His doctrine. For He was teaching them as one having power, and not as the scribes" (Mark 1:22). Christ Himself declared that He was a greater prophet than Jonas: "And behold a greater than Jonas here" (Matthew 12:41). When giving the Jews a new law concerning matrimony, He said that *Moses* had given them one law, but that *He* gave them a new law (Matthew 19:6-7). He even claimed power to interpret God's own law concerning the sabbath: "Therefore," He said, "the Son of Man is Lord of the sabbath also" (Mark 2:28). When He stated a truth, it was not merely a poetic fancy; it was rather a universal and eternal truth which ought to be accepted by men of every nation. His commission to His apostles was that they should go and "teach all nations . . . teaching them to observe all things whatsoever I have commanded you" (Matthew 28:19-20).

CHRIST DESCRIBED HIS DOCTRINE AS ESSENTIAL. Not only were the truths taught by Christ

important; they were so essential that everlasting life depended upon man's acceptance of them. Whoever accepted His doctrine was building upon a firm and lasting foundation: "Everyone, therefore, that heareth these My words and doth them, shall be likened to a wise man that built his house upon a rock" (Matthew 7:24). The acceptance of His doctrine would lead the believer to God: "Amen, amen, I say unto you, that he who heareth My word . . . hath life everlasting" (John 5:24). Again He said: "Now this is eternal life, that they may know Thee, the only true God, and Jesus Christ, whom Thou hast sent" (John 17:3). To Martha He said: "He that believeth in Me, although he be dead, shall live" (John 11:25).

Deliberate failure to accept the teaching of Christ would lead to eternal ruin: "He that believeth and is baptized, shall be saved; but he that believeth not shall be condemned" (Mark 16:16).

CHRIST'S WORDS CAME FROM GOD. How does Christ dare to make the salvation of the entire world depend upon His words? Because the truth which He teaches has been revealed by God. He says: "For I have not spoken of Myself; but the Father who sent Me, He gave Me commandment what I should say and what I should speak" (John 12:49).

IS CHRIST THE MESSIAS? We have quoted from all four of the evangelists words actually uttered by Christ in which He claimed to be a divinely appointed legate with supreme authority to teach mankind. One explanation might be that Christ was a madman. This explanation is not borne out by the facts of His life. Another explanation might be that He was deluded into believing that He was the Messias. This explanation is weak, for how could a man as sane, as good, and as balanced as Christ accept such exalted ideas of Himself without any reason or evidence? The final explanation is that what Christ said of Himself is true. The proof that this is the correct explanation will be given in its proper place.

POINTS FOR REVIEW AND DISCUSSION

1. Show that Christ claimed to be a divinely appointed legate.

2. Show that all the people knew of this claim.

3. Show that Christ claimed supreme teaching power.

4. Show that Christ described His doctrine as essential to man's welfare.

5. Show that Christ claimed that His doctrine was revealed by God.

6. Criticize this statement from E. Washburn Hopkins, a non-Catholic writer on the history of religion: "He took the best and truest ideas handed down from of old and made them the supreme test of a religious spirit." Note the twofold implication: (1) that Christ taught nothing but what had previously been taught; (2) that He felt free to threaten unbelievers with severe penalties because what He taught was very old and very sacred.

THE NEXT LESSON

Did Christ claim to be more than a divinely appointed legate? This will be the subject of our next lesson.

CHAPTER TWENTY - NINE

CHRIST'S CLAIM TO DIVINITY

**STILL GREATER CLAIM.** As we have said, whatever Christ taught would be true, and would be a thing which we ought to accept, if He were no more than a divinely appointed legate. This He claimed to be. But He claimed far more: He claimed that He Himself was God.

It is amazing, after we have seen how repeatedly and how clearly Christ makes this claim, that anyone should doubt that He made it. Yet such is the case. Even Protestant clergymen, who earn their living by preaching Christ to the people, do not always believe that He claimed to be God. Many are the strange explanations which are given of the words of Scripture in which Christ declares who and what He is. Let us examine these words ourselves, and see what conclusion should be drawn.

CHRIST CLAIMED TO HAVE ETERNAL EXISTENCE. Referring to Himself, Christ said to the Jews:

"No man hath ascended into heaven but He that descended from heaven, the Son of Man who is in heaven" (John 3:13).

On another occasion Christ had told the Jews that Abraham had rejoiced to know of Him. The Jews scoffingly said: "Thou art not yet fifty years old, and hast Thou seen Abraham?" What did Christ answer? He said: "Amen, amen, I say to you, before Abraham was made, I am" (John 8:57-58). The Jews fully understood the meaning of these words, for they took up stones to cast at Him as a blasphemer.

On still another occasion Christ claimed to have existed many centuries before Abraham. In that most beautiful prayer which He made to the Father before beginning His passion, He said: "Now glorify Thou Me, O Father, with Thyself, with the glory which I had, before the world was, with Thee" (John 17:5). Here Christ claims to have existed *before the world was made,* before the very first man was made. He existed before time began, for there was no such thing as time before the world was made.

He did not claim to be an angel, but He was present when the angels fell; for He said: "I saw Satan like lightning falling from heaven" (Luke 10:18). Who is this person who existed before man was made, and who witnessed the fall of the angels, though not an angel Himself? Only one interpretation is possible: He was God. And this was the interpretation placed upon His words by those who heard them.

CHRIST CLAIMED TO BE GOD. In all the words of Christ there is a certain divine dignity and authority. It

"And He said to them: 'I saw Satan like lightning falling from heaven'" (Luke 10:18). . . . "Amen, amen I say to you, before Abraham was made, I am" (John 8:58).

could be shown from innumerable passages that He spoke and acted as God. But we will confine ourselves to four passages in the Gospels in which He clearly and explicitly claimed to be divine.

The first was the occasion when Jesus went to the Feast of the Dedication in Jerusalem. He was in that part of the Temple called Solomon's porch when the Jews gathered around Him and said: "How long dost Thou hold our souls in suspense? If Thou be the Christ, tell us plainly." Jesus would not admit that He had held their souls in suspense. He declared that He had already told them, but that they would not believe. Since they would not believe His words, He said, let them believe the marvelous works by which the Father confirmed His claims. And then He said plainly: "I and the Father are one." Immediately the Jews took up stones to stone Him to death; and when Jesus asked because of which of His good works they stoned Him, they answered: "For a good work we stone Thee not, but for a blasphemy; and because that Thou, being a man, makest Thyself God." And then He showed His divine power by escaping out of their hands. This incident is found in St. John, Chapter 10, verses 22-39.

On an earlier occasion Jesus had asked His apostles who men thought He was. After they had told Him what other men said, He asked who they themselves thought He was. St. Peter, always the most impetuous when there was question of devotion to the Master, said: "Thou art Christ, the Son of the living God" (Matthew 16:16). What a tremendous declaration! What ought Jesus to have done if these words were not true? He should immediately have reproved St. Peter. He should have said: "No, I am not God, but only one who is trying to teach men how to serve God." But He said nothing of the kind. On the contrary, He said: "Blessed art thou, Simon Bar-Jona, because flesh and blood hath not revealed it to thee, but My Father who is in heaven" (Matthew 16:17).

The third occasion on which Christ affirmed His divinity was when He was on trial for His life. He was standing, under oath, before the high priest. Many witnesses were present. Clerks were there, according to Jewish custom, to keep a record of the testimony. The high priest, therefore, addressed Jesus and said: " 'Art thou the Christ, the Son of the blessed God?' " (Mark 14:61). Jesus, who had kept silence while the witnesses were bearing false testimony against Him, spoke when the official representative of the Jewish law thus interrogated Him. He answered: " 'I am. And you shall see the Son of Man sitting on the right hand of the power of God, and coming with the clouds of heaven.' Then the high priest, rending his garments, saith: 'What need we any further witnesses? You have heard the blasphemy. What think you?' Who all condemned Him to be guilty of death" (Mark 14:62-64).

And it was because He claimed to be God that He was put to death. The Jews did not wish to give this reason to Pontius Pilate, whose permission for the execution they had to secure. They gave other reasons first; but when Pontius Pilate, with his finely trained Roman mind, brushed aside their foolish charges, they were forced to exclaim: "We have a law, and according to the law He ought to die, because He made Himself the Son of God" (John 19:7).

The fourth occasion on which Jesus affirmed His divinity was at the time of one of His appearances to His apostles after the resurrection. St. Thomas had declared that he would not believe unless he could put his fingers into the wounds in Christ's hands, and his hand into the wound in His side. Christ granted him his wish. No doubt St. Thomas trembled from head to foot as he felt the wounds of the risen Christ. Convinced and overwhelmed, he could utter only these five words: "My Lord, and my God" (John 20:28). Did Jesus correct or reprove him? On the contrary, He confirmed the truth of what St. Thomas had said by declaring: "Because thou hast seen Me, Thomas, thou hast believed. Blessed are they that have not seen, and have believed" (John 20:29).

NATURE OF THESE DECLARATIONS. Again we

have quoted passages from each of the four evangelists. In these passages Christ clearly and positively declares that He is God. In all, thousands of persons must have heard Him make these claims, and many other thousands learned from others that He had made them. The hearers understood exactly what He meant. He was not claiming to be only a legate. He was not claiming to be only a highly favored child of God. He was not claiming, as some modern critics would have us believe, to be only a very devout and pious man with a special insight into God's nature and wishes. He claimed to be God, and His hearers understood Him in precisely that way. There can be no compromise about this matter. If these claims are false, all Christian churches should be closed, and the world should begin again the apparently hopeless task of discovering what God is and what He desires. If these claims are true, every man should plan his life according to the instructions given by Christ.

POINTS FOR REVIEW AND DISCUSSION

1. Show that Christ claimed to have existed before time began.

2. Show from four passages in the Gospels that Christ claimed to be God.

3. If Christ's claims were false, how would you explain the fact that God did not give some very great sign to show that they were false?

4. Prove the falsity of this statement of H. G. Wells:

"Now it is a matter of fact that in the gospels all that body of theological assertion which constitutes Christianity finds little support. . . . Except for one or two passages in St. John's Gospel it is difficult to get any words actually ascribed to Jesus in which he claimed to be the Jewish Messiah . . . and still more difficult is it to find any claim to be a part of the godhead."

5. Give your opinion of the following statement of George Herbert Betts:

"Through prayer and communion he [Jesus] came so close to God that he could say: 'I and the Father are one.' With unfailing confidence he approached God in a one-to-one relationship and then returned refreshed and heartened to the problems of serving others."

6. Consider this second statement of George Herbert Betts:

"Modern men have quite definitely discarded the idea of demons and all kinds of 'spirits' as actual beings or entities, thus in effect saying that Jesus was mistaken in accepting the common belief of his day in such matters. And, surely, the old order of sin, wickedness, and injustice has not ended, nor has the Son of man returned to the earth in glory to reign over the elect. . . . The unavoidable conclusion is that Jesus expected an event that did not occur."

a. Does the fact that "modern men" entertain a certain idea prove that Jesus was wrong?

b. Was it true that Jesus got His ideas by accepting "the common belief of his day"?

c. Did Jesus ever say that He would return to earth to reign over the elect before the year in which we are now living? What conclusion do you draw from this fact as regards the statement of Mr. Betts?

THE NEXT LESSON

It is one thing to make a claim, and quite another thing to prove it. We have now reached the point where we must see whether or not Christ gave proof of the truth of His claims.

CHAPTER THIRTY

THE CHARACTER
OF CHRIST

IMPORTANCE OF THE SUBJECT. We have now reached the most important proof in apologetics, the proof that Christ was the Messias. It is most important because the truth of the teachings of Christianity depends upon it. Christianity claims that its teachings have come from Christ, and that Christ is the Messias, the Son of God. Christianity has been able to prove from historical documents that it does have the teachings of Christ. But of what value are these doctrines if Christ is not God? If Christ was not God, He was a very great imposter, and His teachings are worth even less than those of Mohammed, Confucius, or John Dowie, for these men at least were not so wicked or so deluded as to claim that they themselves were God.

Christianity, then, must prove that Christ gave evidence for the fact that He is God. Proof or evidence supporting such a claim is of two kinds: (1) internal and (2) external. Internal evidence is that which is found in the character of the person making the claim—in his wisdom, his knowledge, his purity of life, his manifest sincerity, his freedom from delusions. External evidence consists of some sign or mark that can be seen or heard, and that is offered by the person himself or by God in support of the claim. Such signs or marks must of their nature be things that only God can bring to pass; that is, they must be either miracles—visible events surpassing all the powers of nature, or prophecies—the accurate foretelling of future events known only to God.

INTERNAL EVIDENCES OF DIVINITY. In this chapter we will confine ourselves to the internal proof. Internal proof means that there is evidence of the claim right in the character of the one making the claim. When we apply this to the case of Christ, it means that Christ's character itself gives evidence that He was what He claimed to be. Since Christ claimed to be God, His character must give evidence of His being a godlike character, a divine character. Certainly no man who is bad, or has a bad character, can be God. Nor are we to expect just an ordinarily good character, for many men have that. We are to look for a character that is far above what is considered good in an ordinary man—a superhuman character. It is not as easy to prove that *character* is divine as to prove that *works* (miracles and prophecies) are divine. But we can at least show that Christ's character was in harmony with His claims.

But how shall we judge character? The only way by which we can know what kind of character any man has is by what he says and what he does. According as a man speaks and as he acts we speak of him as being either good or bad.

Hence to judge Christ's character we must look (1) at what Christ said; that is, His teachings; and (2) at His actions; that is, His life.

THE TEACHINGS OF CHRIST. It would be impossible here to give a full analysis of the teachings of Christ and to show how these teachings could have come only from the mind of God. However, a general survey will be sufficient to reveal that fact. No mere repetition of adjectives can ever adequately describe His teachings. Only lifelong study can show us their full sublimity, and only intimate acquaintance with His doctrines will begin to bring out their value. In the study of Christ's teachings one fact stands out above all else: they are so sublime that they far surpass the teachings of any man in wisdom and goodness. This means that the doctrines which Christ taught the world contain more wisdom and holiness than those of any other philosopher or religious reformer the world has ever known.

This is the testimony of those living at the time of Christ. Those who listened to Christ—there were thousands of them, friends and enemies—testified that "never did man speak like this man" (John 7:46). History testifies that this opinion of Christ has been held down through the ages to our present day. While there have been many controversies concerning the teachings of Christ, the disputes have never been concerning the *wisdom and holiness* of His teachings, but concerning the *interpretation* of His teachings. Never in the history of Christianity have Christ's doctrines been attacked for lack of superior wisdom or goodness. Even in our present day, in this age of irreligion, men who are enemies to Christianity and disbelievers in Christ's divinity testify to the superhuman character of His doctrines. "The teaching of Jesus is the most beautiful moral teaching which humanity has received. The morality of the gospel is the most beautiful code of perfect life which any moralist has traced" (Renan).

In summarizing what the world has said of the teachings of Christ, we find superhuman wisdom and holiness characterizing His doctrines. But wisdom and holiness are attributes of God. Consequently we are within reason when we say that Christ's teachings are godlike.

But where did Christ get these doctrines? Certainly He did not learn them in any university. Christ never attended any university. There were men living at the time of Christ who knew Christ well. They knew that Christ had never been taught by a human teacher. That was why they cried out in astonishment at His wisdom: "How came this man by this wisdom?" (Matthew 13:54). Since this wisdom did not come from any other man, it must have come from Christ Himself. This is sufficient to prove the character of Christ's mind: at least, it was superhuman and godlike.

THE LIFE OF CHRIST. What a terrible revelation it would be of Christ's character to find that He taught one doctrine but practiced another! If such a thing were true, Christ would be immediately branded as an imposter. Christ claimed He was God. To prove that fact Christ must not only talk as God talks, but He must also act as God acts. Since Christ's doctrines are godlike, His actions ought to be in accordance with His doctrines. Christ told others: "Be ye perfect as your heavenly Father is perfect." We ought, then, to find Christ leading a perfect life.

That Christ did live a perfect life is the testimony of those who knew Him—even His enemies. When Christ was before the court of Pilate, Pilate was forced to tell the Jews: "I find no cause in Him" (John 19:6). It must be remembered that Christ was condemned to death not because of any wrongdoing, but because He claimed to be the Son of God.

Moreover, history has never found anything concerning Christ that would be opposed to a life of perfection. On the contrary, page after page of the Gospels is filled with examples of superhuman perfection in Christ. This historical document testifies that Christ's life was most exemplary and in perfect accord with His teachings. His acts of kindness, generosity, humility, patience, modesty, and meekness prove beyond reasonable doubt that He led a perfect life, a life that was in harmony with His doctrines and with the nature of God. Most certainly, then, Christ gave positive internal evidence of His claim to divinity and Messiahship.

POINTS FOR REVIEW AND DISCUSSION

1. In what two ways should we judge Christ's character?

2. As concerns the sublimity of Christ's teachings, give testimony from (1) men of His own day, (2) later generations, (3) modern times.

3. Describe an event in the life of Christ when He was quite young (not mentioned in this chapter) which confirms our statement that Christ did not acquire His wisdom in any school.

4. Show that even Christ's enemies admitted the perfection of His life.

5. Make a list of all the virtues of which you can think, and show how they were practiced by Christ.

6. What argument can be drawn from the fact that the very wisest and holiest men and women of all ages since the time of Christ have endeavored in vain to imitate perfectly His virtues?

THE NEXT LESSON

The proof provided by the miracles of Christ will be the subject of the next lesson.

CHAPTER THIRTY-ONE

THE MIRACLES
OF CHRIST

PROVING FORCE OF MIRACLES. A miracle, as we have said, is a visible event which surpasses all the powers of nature. It is true that we do not know everything that nature can do; we are constantly discovering new forces in nature by using which we accomplish wonderful things. But although we do not know everything that nature *can do,* we know certain things that nature *cannot do.* If you have broken your arm, and the X-ray shows that the bone is broken in two pieces and badly splintered, you know that no power in nature can completely heal that arm in a second. Possibly five hundred years from now some force in nature will have been discovered which can bring about such a result. The physician who discovers it will be remembered forever. But if such a force exists, steps will have to be taken *to apply it to broken arms,* just as steps have to be taken to use those forces in nature which make it possible for us to transmit sound by radio. If the force existed in nature and worked, as gravitation does, without any effort on the part of man, it would heal broken arms regularly, or at least frequently. It follows that we can know without any fear of error that certain events are not due to any force in nature. If they are not due to any force in nature, they must be due to God.

We can divide the miracles of Christ into three classes: (1) those involving power over the physical properties of bodies, (2) the healing of the sick, and (3) the raising of the dead to life.

MIRACLES OF THE FIRST TYPE. We will mention some of these miracles briefly, for with far greater miracles with which to prove our point, there is no need to discuss these miracles in detail. Some of the most striking among them are as follows:

1. At the marriage feast in Cana Christ turned water into wine (John 2:1-11).

2. He so multiplied five loaves and two fish that five thousand men, and an unknown number of women and children, had enough to eat (Matthew 14:14-21).

3. He walked upon the waters of the sea without sinking (Mark 6:48-51).

4. After the apostles had fished all night without catching anything, He caused their net to be so filled with fish that it broke (Luke 5:4-10).

THE HEALING OF THE SICK. On numerous occasions Christ healed the sick and cured those who were defective or maimed. The following may be mentioned as examples of miracles of this type:

1. Leprosy is incurable even today, despite all the advances of science. On one occasion He cured a leper by a mere word; on another occasion He cured ten (Matthew 8:2-3; Luke 17:12-19).

2. He cured a man who was afflicted with paralysis (Matthew 9:2-8). As if to anticipate the objections of those critics who say that paralysis may disappear because of sudden excitement, He cured the servant of the centurion at a great distance and without seeing or speaking to him (Matthew 8:5-13).

3. He cured at least seven blind persons (Matthew 9:27-31, 12:22, 20:30-34; Mark 8:22-26, 10:46-52; Luke 18:35-43; John 9:1-7).

4. He cured in an instant a person suffering from a violent fever (Luke 4:38-39).

5. He restored hearing and speech to a deaf mute (Mark 7:32-35).

These are but a few examples. The evangelists on more than one occasion tell us that Christ cured of diverse diseases *all* those who were brought to Him.

THE CASE OF THE MAN BORN BLIND. We must never forget that it is not necessary for us to prove that Christ worked *many* miracles. One undoubted miracle for which there is ample evidence is all that we need. Let us, then, take one of these cures and examine it in greater detail. We will select one which Christ said He intended to be a proof of His divine power. It is the cure of the man born blind, described in the ninth chapter of St. John. Let us study it point by point.

1. Jesus worked this miracle to show His divine power, and He deliberately worked it on the sabbath as an object lesson to the Pharisees, who attached more importance to the servile observance of the law than they did to true brotherly love. This is apparent as we read through the story, which begins as follows:

And Jesus, passing by, saw a man who was blind from his birth. And His disciples asked Him: "Rabbi, who hath sinned, this man or his parents, that he should be born blind?" Jesus answered: "Neither hath this man sinned, nor his parents; but that the works of God should be made manifest in him. I must work the works of Him that sent Me whilst it is day; the night cometh, when no man can work. As long as I am in the world, I am the light of the world." When He had said these things, He spat on the ground, and made clay of the spittle, and spread the clay upon his eyes. And said to him: "Go, wash in the pool of Siloe" (which is interpreted, Sent). He went, therefore, and washed, and he came seeing (John 9:1-7).

2. The blind man's neighbors were so amazed by the miracle that they could scarcely believe that the cured man, now going about in a perfectly normal manner, was the former blind beggar.

The neighbors, therefore, and they who had seen him before that [when] he was a beggar, said: "Is not this he that sat and begged?" Some said: "This is he," but others said: "No, but he is like him." But he said: "I am he." They said, therefore, to him: "How were thy eyes opened?" He answered: "That man that is called Jesus made clay and anointed my eyes, and said to me: 'Go to the pool of Siloe and wash.' And I went, I washed, and I see" (John 9:8-11).

3. Now, the neighbors undoubtedly knew how opposed

the Pharisees were to Jesus. They feared the Pharisees, and so they thought that the most prudent thing to do would be to refer the whole case to them. The Pharisees, as usual, refused to believe the evidence of their senses, but the blind man courageously declared that Jesus must be a prophet.

And they said to him: "Where is He?" He saith: "I know not." They bring him that had been blind to the Pharisees. Now it was the sabbath when Jesus made the clay and opened his eyes. Again, therefore, the Pharisees asked him how he had received his sight. But he said to them: "He put clay upon my eyes, and I washed, and I see." Some, therefore, of the Pharisees said: "This man is not of God, who keepeth not the sabbath." But others said: "How can a man that is a sinner do such miracles?" And there was a division among them. They say, therefore, to the blind man again: "What sayest thou of Him that hath opened thy eyes?" And he said: "He is a prophet" (John 9:12-17).

4. It is difficult even today to educate blind persons. In those days, when few persons were highly educated, it was still more difficult. The poor beggar who had been blind from birth could not have been a very highly educated or cultured person; but he had enough intelligence to know that only God could have opened his eyes. He saw the truth because he was willing to see it; the Pharisees on their part were not willing to see it. Desperately determined to do away with this manifest miracle if they could, they sent for the man's parents. The parents obeyed the summons, but were careful to keep out of trouble themselves.

The Jews, then, did not believe concerning him that he had been blind and had received his sight, until they called the parents of him that had received his sight, and asked them, saying: "Is this

"*He spat on the ground, and made clay of the spittle, and spread the clay upon his eyes. And said to him: 'Go, wash in the pool of Siloe.' . . . He went, therefore, and washed, and he came seeing*" (John 9:6-7).

your son, who you say was born blind? How, then, doth he now see?" His parents answered them and said: "We know that this is our son, and that he was born blind. But how he now seeth, we know not; or who hath opened his eyes, we know not. Ask himself; he is of age, let him speak for himself." These things his parents said because they feared the Jews; for the Jews had already agreed among themselves that, if any man should confess Him to be Christ, he should be put out of the synagogue. Therefore did his parents say: "He is of age, ask himself" (John 9:18-23).

5. By this time it was simply impossible for the Pharisees to doubt that the blind man had been cured, and that he had been cured by Jesus. But they were still determined to find some explanation. They knew, so they said, that Jesus was a sinner—just as persons 'know' today, without any evidence, that God does not exist or that the Catholic Church is not the Church of Christ. So they sent once more for the blind man, who by this time had begun to realize more clearly what had happened to him.

They therefore called the man again that had been blind, and said to him: "Give glory to God. We know that this man is a sinner." He said, therefore, to them: "If He be a sinner, I know not. One thing I know, that whereas I was blind, now I see." They said, then, to him: "What did He to thee? How did He open thy eyes?" He answered them: "I have told you already, and you have heard. Why would you hear it again? Will you also become His disciples?" They reviled him, therefore, and said: "Be thou His disciple, but we are the disciples of Moses. We know that God spoke to Moses; but as to this man, we know not from whence He is." The man answered and said to them: "Why, herein is a wonderful thing, that you know not from whence He is, and He hath opened my eyes. Now, we know that God doth not hear sinners; but if a man be a server of God and doth His will, him He heareth.

From the beginning of the world it hath not been heard that any man hath opened the eyes of one born blind. Unless this man were of God, He could not do anything." They answered and said to him: "Thou wast wholly born in sins, and dost thou teach us?" And they cast him out (John 9:24-34).

6. Now comes the climax of the story. Light had been offered to the Pharisees, but they had refused it. The humble blind man, despite the danger to himself, confesses that Christ is God. Christ permits him to fall upon his knees and adore Him as God.

Jesus heard that they had cast him out. And when He had found him, He said to him: "Dost thou believe in the Son of God?" He answered and said: "Who is He, Lord, that I may believe in Him?" And Jesus said to him: "Thou hast both seen Him, and it is He that talketh with thee." And he said: "I believe, Lord." And falling down, he adored Him (John 9:35-38).

This, then, was the miracle of the restoration of sight to the blind man. It actually happened; it was a thing surpassing all the forces of nature; it was carefully verified by hostile witnesses; and it was offered by Christ as a proof of His divinity.

THE RAISING OF LAZARUS. Jesus raised several persons from the dead, but the most striking of these miracles is that of the raising of Lazarus, described in the eleventh chapter of St. John. Lazarus had been dead for four days, and his sister Martha did not wish to have the tomb opened because she knew his body must have begun to corrupt. But the stone was taken away, and when Jesus had called upon Lazarus with a loud voice, he came forth, bound feet and hands with winding bands, and his face bound about with a napkin. And Jesus, before working this miracle, had raised His eyes to heaven and told the heavenly Father that He intended to work it in proof of His divine mission.

FALSE EXPLANATIONS. All attempts of unbelievers to explain away these miracles can be grouped under two heads: (1) the miracles never took place, or (2) they were due to natural causes.

If these miracles never took place, the four evangelists were liars of the most unscrupulous kind. Is it not true that it becomes far more difficult for us to tell a lie if we give a great many details instead of simply making one short statement? For example, it is not so difficult for us to excuse ourselves for getting home late by saying that the teacher kept us after school, when as a matter of fact no such thing happened; but if we begin to go further by inventing numerous details, telling what the teacher did and what we did, what the teacher said and what we said, we realize far more vividly that we are lying in an inexcusable way. This is what the evangelists would have had to do. They would have been in the position of deliberately inventing stories and palming them off as true.

But if they did invent stories, how can we explain the fact that in many cases these four men, writing independently, invented the *same* story? True, some explanation for such a thing could be imagined, but it would not be a very probable one, and it would not have any real evidence to support it.

Moreover, when men begin to invent stories of miracles, they are very apt to invent something grotesque and incredible. The miracles of the Gospels are not of this kind.

Again, the apostles referred to these miracles immediately after the resurrection of Christ and among the very people where the miracles were said to have occurred. In some cases (see Mark 10:46) the names of those involved in the miracles were given. Christ, after His own resurrection, remained invisible except when He wished to manifest Himself; but Lazarus after his raising from the dead could be seen and questioned by all, and in fact we are told that many of the Jews did go to visit him. If these miracles had not really taken place, the apostles would merely have made themselves the laughing-stock of their hearers instead of converting thousands of Jews to the faith.

Finally, the disciples of Christ in general were slow to believe. Christ reproached His apostles for this. St. Thomas refused to believe that Christ had risen from the dead until he felt His wounds with his own hand. Just as there is no evidence whatsoever to justify the belief that the evangelists were deliberate liars, so likewise there is no evidence to prove that they were empty-headed dreamers who readily believed fairy tales.

Then there is the objection that the miracles were due to physical causes. In particular, it is said that they were faith cures—that persons were cured because of the powerful influence exerted on them by the personality and reputation of Christ.

It is true that cures may sometimes be due to causes such

as this, especially when the disease is nervous rather than organic. But Christ wrought cures under three circumstances which exclude any possibility of this kind of influence:

First, when the patient was at a great distance from Him, as when He cured the servant of the centurion (Matthew 8:5-13).

Secondly, when the patient was deaf, dumb, and blind (Matthew 12:22).

Thirdly, when the patient was dead (John 11:1-45).

Of what benefit is it to the enemies of Christ to declare that some of His miracles *may have been due* to the nervous excitement and faith of the one who was cured? This at best is a mere possibility, a mere conjecture. But even if we accepted it as a fact, there would still remain miracles which could not be explained in this way, and one clear-cut miracle is all that is necessary to prove Christ's claim.

POINTS FOR REVIEW AND DISCUSSION

1. Name the three classes into which the miracles of Christ can be divided.

2. Name some miracles falling in the first class.

3. Name some miracles falling in the second class.

4. Describe a miracle falling in the third class.

5. Answer the charge that the miracle stories in the Gospels are myths.

6. Answer the charge that the miracles were due to natural causes.

7. Consider the following passage from the non-Catholic E. Washburn Hopkins:

THE MIRACLES OF CHRIST

"Jesus is represented as performing miracles, some of which would be accepted today as due to the curative power of a strong spirituality, while others came in response to the usual Eastern demand for marvels, which have always been required of a religious leader. Jesus himself deprecated such signs and the Biblical narrative intimates that they were often the result of subjective belief: Mark vi:5: 'He could do there no mighty work'; because of their unbelief, Matt. xiii:58."

a. Faith cures are cures which come about because of the intense conviction of the sick person that he is going to get well. There is no need to deny that they occur. Possibly some cures mentioned in the Gospels were of this kind. Show that this would not weaken our argument.

b. Mr. Hopkins says that some miracles "came in response to the usual Eastern demand for marvels." Show the truth of the following propositions: (1) If Mr. Hopkins means that Jesus actually worked miracles, He would still be God whether or not He did so in response to an Eastern demand. (2) If he means that the evangelists invented the miracle stories to satisfy this demand, he is making a purely arbitrary and unsupported charge which we have already refuted.

c. When Mr. Hopkins says that Jesus deprecated such signs, he must refer to the fact that Jesus reproached men for being unwilling to believe unless they saw miracles. Show that this does not create a difficulty.

d. The quotation from Matthew 13:58 reads differently in the Douay version, which says: "And He wrought not many miracles there, because of their unbelief." But take Mr. Hopkins' version as it stands, and show that it proves nothing against the divinity of Christ.

e. Which of the statements made by Mr. Hopkins are shown to be false or misleading by the raising of Lazarus from the dead, and particularly by what Jesus says in John 11:41-42?

8. Do miracles occur today? Can you describe any of the recent

miracles at Lourdes and the precautions taken to verify the fact that they are real miracles? What is the official attitude of the Church toward all such apparent miracles? What should be our attitude toward present-day miracles?

THE NEXT LESSON

The next lesson will take up the greatest of all the miracles of Christ, His own resurrection.

THE RESURRECTION OF CHRIST

JESUS UNDOUBTEDLY DIED UPON THE CROSS. There can be no doubt about the fact that Jesus died upon the cross. St. Matthew tells us that "Jesus, again crying out with a loud voice, yielded up the ghost" (Matthew 27:50). The three other evangelists likewise declare that Jesus died (Mark 15:37; Luke 23:46; John 19:30). The soldiers, seeing that Jesus was already dead, did not break His legs (John 19:33). Pontius Pilate would not give the body of Jesus to Joseph of Arimathea until he had sent a centurion to make certain that Jesus had expired (Mark 15:44-45). And if Jesus had not been already dead, He would have died when the soldier pierced His side with a lance, leaving a wound so great that St. Thomas was later able to place his hand within it (John 19:34, 20:27).

JESUS HAD PREDICTED HIS RESURRECTION. But Jesus had declared that He would rise again from the dead. It was after He had announced to His apostles that He intended to establish a perpetual Church of which St. Peter would be the head that He prepared them for what was to come by telling them of His death and resurrection. "From that time Jesus began to show to His disciples that He must go to Jerusalem, and suffer many things from the ancients and scribes and chief priests, and be put to death, and the third day rise again" (Matthew 16:21).

JESUS DID RISE FROM THE DEAD. The resurrection of Christ is described by all four of the evangelists: by St. Matthew in Chapter 28, by St. Mark in Chapter 16, by St. Luke in Chapter 24, and by St. John in Chapter 20. Let us examine their testimony from every point of view.

1. The evangelists were eyewitnesses or equivalently so. St. Matthew and St. John described what they had seen with their own eyes. St. Luke obtained his facts from persons who had themselves seen the Lord after His resurrection. St. Mark was a disciple of St. Peter and wrote his Gospel with St. Peter's approval.

2. The witnesses were sincere and honest men. They were reluctant to believe that Jesus had really risen, and He was forced to go to some lengths to convince them of the fact. True, men can sometimes be so stubborn that they will cling to a position even though they gain nothing in this world or the next; and so it is conceivable that the disciples of Christ, if both He and they had been deceivers of the worst type, might have sought to gain some sort of victory over their enemies by inventing the story of the resurrection. But in the first place such a gross and deliberate deception is not

"For an angel of the Lord descended from heaven, and coming, rolled back the stone, and sat upon it. . . . And for fear of him the guards were struck with terror, and became as dead men" (Matthew 28:2-4).

in harmony with the characters of the evangelists as revealed by their lives and their writings. To be a follower of Christ oftentimes meant death—they saw that in the case of St. Stephen. If the apostles all their lives long lied about the resurrection of Christ, they deserved to be hanged as murderers, for they sent to torture and death hundreds of good men and women who became Christians and died as martyrs because of their preaching. In the second place, it is evident that they did not conspire to invent the story of the resurrection, for after the death of Christ they gave up all hope, went into hiding, and began to disperse.

3. The witnesses had ample opportunity to investigate the truth of the resurrection. Jesus remained on earth for forty days, appearing frequently to individuals and to large groups. He spoke and even ate with them; He permitted them to examine His wounds; and He repeatedly declared that He had indeed risen. That the apostles did investigate the matter for themselves is evident from the fact that they would not believe the women who came to tell them of the resurrection, from the fact that when Jesus first appeared to the eleven apostles (just after the two disciples who had seen Jesus at Emmaus had brought the news to them) they thought that they saw a spirit (Luke 24:37), and from the fact that St. Thomas and some others were so slow to believe that we can scarcely imagine ourselves acting in the same way under the same circumstances. Their doubt destroys the grounds of doubt in our own minds.

4. The enemies of Christ had ample opportunity to investigate the story. On the day of Pentecost, less than two

months after Christ's resurrection, St. Peter told the story publicly to a very large number of Jews. There can be no doubt that the Jews did everything they could to discredit the story. But the best story *they* could invent was that the disciples had stolen the body of Jesus from the tomb. The Jews had in fact given a great sum of money to the soldiers who had been sent to guard the tomb, bribing them to say that the disciples had come while they were asleep and taken away the body. As St. Augustine says, these were indeed poor witnesses; they testified to what happened while they were asleep, and they must have been heavy sleepers not to awake when the disciples came and removed from the sepulcher the very heavy stone which had been rolled against the door. The apostles made many converts in Jerusalem immediately after Pentecost, and they made them by preaching to the people the risen Christ. Must we not believe that these converts, who were risking their very lives by becoming Christians, asked for proof that Christ had risen? Were the apostles and disciples deliberately lying when they said: "We saw Him with our own eyes"? This is something which we cannot believe.

CHRIST ROSE IN PROOF OF HIS DIVINITY.

On one occasion the Jews asked Jesus for a sign. Jesus promised that He would give them a sign. He said: "As Jonas was in the whale's belly three days and three nights, so shall the Son of Man be in the heart of the earth three days and three nights" (Matthew 12:40). On still another occasion when the Jews asked for a sign, Jesus said: "Destroy this temple, and in three days I will raise it up" (John 2:19).

Christ, therefore, appealed to His resurrection as a proof of His divinity.

Earlier in this book we used our reason to prove that God exists, that He created man for a purpose, and that He exercises providence over the world which He made. Let us now think for a moment of what God was doing in heaven while all these events were happening on earth. If Jesus Christ was truly God, we can easily imagine what was happening: God was looking down with approval and doing His part to carry the work forward. But what if Jesus Christ was not truly God? What if the Blessed Sacrament, which we adore as God, is nothing but a piece of bread? What would God be doing then? He would be doing nothing while Jesus Christ and a little group of men were putting together the greatest historical deception, or suffering the greatest delusion, which ever occurred or could ever be imagined. The result was to be that billions of the best minds of the world for centuries thereafter would adore a false god. Not only would they adore a false god, but the evidence proving to them that they should adore this false god was to be so complete and perfect that the keenest intellect could find no real flaw in it. Could God permit this? Could He simply do nothing while this great fraud was being built up? Why did He not strike Jesus Christ dead? Why did He not cause something to occur which would show that Jesus Christ was not what He claimed to be?

The fact that God did nothing of the kind confirms the truth of the resurrection and of Christ's claim that He was divine.

THE RESURRECTION OF CHRIST

POINTS FOR REVIEW AND DISCUSSION

1. Show that Christ predicted His resurrection.

2. Prove the reliability of the testimony to the effect that Christ rose from the dead.

3. Tell how Christ appealed to His resurrection as a proof of His claims.

4. Show that the body of the risen Christ was a real human body.

5. Why could not the devil have made the disciples think that they saw Christ's risen body?

6. In a number of pagan religions gods were represented as having risen from the dead. If you were to go to some non-Catholic university, you might very possibly hear some professor declare that the evangelists, in putting into writing the resurrection myth, were drawing upon old legends. How would you answer an objection such as this?

7. It is incredible to what lengths men will go when they have once determined not to believe that Jesus was divine. State your opinion of these words of George Herbert Betts, in which he declares that Jesus becomes a better leader and model if we deprive Him of His divinity:

"But if we believe that Jesus, because of a unique relation to God, was so equipped that he could not fail, and that every battle was won before it was begun, then there seems an element of injustice in expecting us with our lesser equipment to approximate the level he reached."

8. The same George Herbert Betts says:

"Again, what difference will it make in one's conduct, his outlook upon life, his loyalty to the Christian ideal if he believes in the physical resurrection of Jesus as against believing that Jesus escaped from death only through the immortality of his spirit, which lives even now to bless the world? Are not beliefs on such questions incidental when measured by the test of *the way they function* in experience?"

In answer to the position here taken by Mr. Betts, show what we would have to believe about God and the possibility of knowing His will with certainty if Jesus did not rise from the dead. Show how belief in the resurrection *does* affect the conduct and the outlook upon life of a good Catholic.

9. Examine into the proofs offered by H. G. Wells in the passage which follows, and state what you think of them:

"The souls of the disciples were plunged for a time into utter darkness. Then presently came a whisper among them and stories, rather discrepant stories, that the body of Jesus was not in the tomb in which it had been placed, and that first one and then another had seen him alive. Soon they were consoling themselves with the conviction that he had risen from the dead, that he had shown himself to many, and had ascended visibly into heaven. Witnesses were found to declare that they had positively seen him go up, visibly in his body. He had gone through the blue—to God."

THE NEXT LESSON

We have proved Christ's divinity from His character and from His miracles. One point only remains: the proof from the prophecies.

CHAPTER THIRTY-THREE

THE PROPHECIES

DIVINE KNOWLEDGE RE-QUIRED FOR PROPHE-CIES. A prophecy, which is the certain and definite prediction of a future event, especially of an event involving the free action of God or man, requires divine knowledge, for only God can foresee with certainty what will be freely done in the future. It is not a prophecy to foretell that an eclipse will take place at a certain time, for an eclipse is due to natural laws which are understood by man. Nor would it be a prophecy to declare that another European war will occur within twenty-five years; for if those who prophesy such a thing prove to be right, it will be because they have correctly estimated those social forces which lead nations toward peace or toward war. It is different when the thing foretold is due neither to natural nor to social forces, for in that case only God can know with certainty that it is to occur.

It follows from this that the prophecies made concerning Christ centuries before His birth must have been revealed by God. If God revealed them, He put His seal of approval upon Christ. As for the prophecies made by Christ Himself, they likewise are proofs of divine power and confirm whatever claims He made.

PROPHECIES CONCERNING CHRIST. The Old Testament is so full of prophecies concerning Christ that we can do no more than describe them in a general way and mention some of the more striking ones.

In general, Christ is described as follows:

1. He is God.
2. He is the Anointed One.
3. He belongs to the house of David.
4. He is king, shepherd, priest, and redeemer.
5. He is just, mild, and the Prince of Peace.
6. He will overcome all His enemies.
7. He will abolish the Old Law.
8. His kingdom will be spiritual, universal, and eternal.

This composite description is taken from many passages in the Old Testament. One passage which includes almost all the ideas here given is as follows: "For a child is born to us and a son is given to us, and the government is upon His shoulder; and His name shall be called Wonderful, Counselor, God the Mighty, the Father of the World to Come, the Prince of Peace" (Isaias 9:6).

In particular, certain events in the life of Christ were clearly predicted:

1. The preaching of St. John the Baptist. "Behold, I send My angel [messenger], and he shall prepare the way before My face. And presently the Lord, whom you seek, and the

angel of the testament, whom you desire, shall come to His temple" (Malachias 3:1).

2. The birth of Christ of a virgin mother. "The Lord Himself shall give you a sign. Behold, a virgin shall conceive and bear a son, and His name shall be called Emmanuel" (Isaias 7:14).

3. The birth of Christ in Bethlehem. This was the prophecy which enabled the priests to tell the Three Kings where to look for Jesus. "And thou, Bethlehem Ephrata, art a little one among the thousands of Juda; out of thee shall He come forth unto Me that is to be the ruler in Israel, and His going forth is from the beginning, from the days of eternity" (Micheas 5:2).

4. The residence of Christ in Egypt. "I called My Son out of Egypt" (Osee 11:1).

5. The entrance of Jesus into Jerusalem on Palm Sunday. "Behold, thy King will come to thee, the just and Saviour; He is poor, and riding upon an ass, and upon a colt the foal of an ass" (Zacharias 9:9).

6. The betrayal of Jesus for thirty pieces of silver. "And they weighed for My wages thirty pieces of silver" (Zacharias 11:12).

7. The flight of the apostles when Jesus was taken prisoner. "Strike the shepherd, and the sheep shall be scattered" (Zacharias 13:7).

8. The death of Christ and His prayer for His executioners. "He hath delivered His soul unto death, and was reputed with the wicked; and He hath borne the sins of many, and hath prayed for the transgressors" (Isaias 53:12).

9. The violence of Christ's persecutors. "I have given My body to the strikers and My cheeks to them that plucked them; I have not turned away My face from them that rebuked Me and spit upon Me" (Isaias 50:6).

10. The gall and vinegar which Christ was given to drink. "And they gave Me gall for My food, and in My thirst they gave Me vinegar to drink" (Psalm 68:22).

11. The wounds of Christ. "They have dug My hands and feet. They have numbered all My bones" (Psalm 21:17-18).

12. The dividing up of Christ's garments by the soldiers. "They parted My garments amongst them, and upon My vesture they cast lots" (Psalm 21:19).

PROPHECIES MADE BY CHRIST. Christ Himself made the following prophecies:

1. He predicted His passion, death, and resurrection. "Behold, we go up to Jerusalem, and the Son of Man shall be betrayed to the chief priests and the scribes, and they shall condemn Him to death. And shall deliver Him to the Gentiles to be mocked and scourged, and crucified, and the third day He shall rise again" (Matthew 20:18-19).

2. He predicted the treason of Judas. " 'Amen, I say to you, that one of you is about to betray Me. . . .' And Judas that betrayed Him, answering, said, 'Is it I, Rabbi?' He saith to him: 'Thou hast said it' " (Matthew 26:21-25).

3. He predicted His desertion by the apostles. "And Jesus saith to them: 'You will all be scandalized in My regard this night. For it is written: 'I will strike the shepherd, and the sheep shall be dispersed' " (Mark 14:27).

4. He predicted St. Peter's denial. "And Jesus saith to him: 'Amen, I say to thee, today, even in this night, before the cock crow twice, thou shalt deny Me thrice'" (Mark 14:30).

5. He predicted the destruction of Jerusalem. "And they shall not leave in thee a stone upon a stone, because that thou hast not known the time of thy visitation" (Luke 19:44).

6. He predicted the persecutions which His apostles would suffer. "They will deliver you up in councils, and they will scourge you in their synagogues. And you shall be brought before governors and before kings for My sake, for a testimony to them and to the Gentiles" (Matthew 10:17-18).

7. He predicted the perpetual existence of His Church. "Behold, I am with you all days, even to the consummation of the world" (Matthew 28:20). This prophecy has not yet been completely fulfilled, but the existence of the Church after nineteen centuries of trial is an indication that it will be.

THE PROPHECIES AS PROOF. After predicting the treason of Judas, Jesus said: "At present I tell you, before it come to pass, that when it shall come to pass, you may believe that I am He" (John 13:19). He also stated on more than one occasion that the prophets of the Old Testament had written concerning Him. And indeed, to whom could these old prophecies refer if not to Christ? These prophets, writing centuries apart, gave many details concerning Christ which fit Him perfectly and which fit no one else. Heaven has thus confirmed in every possible way the truth of His divinity.

POINTS FOR REVIEW AND DISCUSSION

1. Mention some of the prophecies of the Old Testament concerning Christ, and show that they were fulfilled in Him.

2. Mention the prophecies made by Christ, and tell whether they were fulfilled.

3. We know that at the time of Christ the Jews were convinced that He would soon appear. This expectation was due to a large extent to the prophecy of Daniel. Daniel lived at a time when the Jews were in captivity and when Jerusalem had been completely destroyed. But he saw three things in vision: (1) the rebuilding of Jerusalem; (2) the coming of Christ; and (3) the destruction of Jerusalem after the death of Christ. Let us examine into this prophecy.

a. "Know thou therefore and take notice, that from the going forth of the word to build up Jerusalem again unto Christ the prince, there shall be seven weeks and sixty-two weeks" (Daniel 9:25).

"The going forth of the word to build up Jerusalem again" was the decree of Artaxerxes in 456 B. C.

A "week" was a week of years, or seven years.

Christ was not born in the precise year when He was thought to have been born at the time that the calendar was revised. His birth probably took place in the year 4 B. C., and His manifestation to the world at the beginning of His public life took place about the year A. D. 27.

On the basis of these facts, discuss the accuracy of Daniel's prophecy.

b. Daniel then continues: "And after sixty-two weeks Christ shall be slain, and the people that shall deny Him shall not be

THE PROPHECIES

His" (Daniel 9:26). There is nothing here that requires study. We might, however, explain one thing. When Daniel said that there would be "seven weeks and sixty-two weeks," it is thought he meant that there would be seven weeks till the rebuilding of Jerusalem, and then sixty-two weeks from the rebuilding of Jerusalem to Christ. "After sixty-two weeks" means, therefore, the same thing as "after seven weeks and sixty-two weeks" so far as our computations are concerned.

c. "And a people with their leader that shall come, shall destroy the city and the sanctuary" (Daniel 9:26). Could this refer to the destruction of Jerusalem by the Romans under Titus?

d. "And He shall confirm the covenant with many in one week. And in the half of the week the victim and the sacrifice shall fail; and there shall be in the temple the abomination of desolation, and the desolation shall continue even to the consummation and to the end" (Daniel 9:27).

A week is seven years. Does the condition in which the Church was seven years after Christ began His public life prove the truth of the first sentence quoted in (d)?

The old Jewish sacrifices were abolished when Christ died upon the cross. What does the prophecy say concerning the time when the victim and the sacrifice would cease to be?

Has the last part of the prophecy been verified?

THE NEXT LESSON

We have now completed the proof of the divinity of Christ. One thing only remains, and that is to learn what Christ desires us to do in order to fulfill His wishes and to profit by the work which He came to accomplish.

CHAPTER THIRTY-FOUR

JESUS CHRIST FOUNDED A CHURCH

 **AS A CHURCH ABSO-
LUTELY NECESSARY?**
You have read in the third chapter of
Genesis how God spoke to Adam and
Eve after their fall and promised them a
redeemer. It is also possible that He told them other things
about Himself which are not recorded in Scripture. This is
what is known as 'primitive revelation,' and we find traces
of it in the history of many ancient races. Men knew something, both from their own reason and from the truths
handed down to them, about the manner in which they
ought to worship and serve God.

But until the establishment of the Jewish nation many
centuries later, there was no official organization, no church,
to which men could turn for an answer to their religious
difficulties. God revealed Himself at times to certain individuals—to Noe, for example—but there was no universal
church with authority to teach and govern in spiritual matters the entire world.

Just as God in the beginning made a revelation to man and then left man to work out his salvation without assistance from any world-wide organization, so likewise Jesus Christ might have returned to heaven without leaving behind Him a church appointed to carry on His work. The question now is, what did Jesus Christ actually do? What do the records say? Does He wish men living today to do the best they can to interpret for themselves the lessons of His life, or did He establish a church possessing authority from God to tell them what they ought to do?

JESUS CHRIST FOUNDED A CHURCH. It is evident that Jesus Christ intended to establish an organization. For first of all He encouraged men to follow Him and to remain in His company. "A great multitude followed Him," says St. John (John 6:2). To one man He said: "Follow Me, and let the dead bury their dead" (Matthew 8:22). To the young man desirous of learning how to be perfect He said: "Sell whatsoever thou hast . . . and come, follow Me" (Mark 10:21). From among those who thus followed Him, He selected large groups, and sent them, after He had given them special instructions, to preach the Gospel to others. "And after these things the Lord appointed also other seventy-two, and He sent them two and two before His face into every city and place whither He Himself was to come" (Luke 10:1).

In particular, He selected twelve men who were to remain with Him most constantly and to be specially instructed in His doctrine. These men were trained for a definite work. "Come after Me," He said, "and I will make you to become fishers of men" (Mark 1:17). The night before He died, He said to these same men: "And you shall give testimony, because you are with Me from the beginning" (John 15:27).

Jesus, then, was not like a popular orator who goes about from place to place exhorting or instructing the people, but leaving no organization behind him. He gathered men around Him and gave them a specific work to do. This is what we mean by founding an organization. He wished all men to belong to this organization: "Other sheep I have . . . them also I must bring . . . and there shall be one fold and one shepherd" (John 10:16).

HIS CHURCH WAS SPIRITUAL. This organization

was to be a spiritual organization, not a worldly or political one. It was for the benefit of men's souls. "Be you therefore perfect, as also your heavenly Father is perfect," He said (Matthew 5:48). Again He said: "If any man will follow Me, let him deny himself, and take up his cross" (Mark 8:34). His organization was to be in the state, but not the same as the state; "Render therefore to Caesar the things that are Caesar's, and to God the things that are God's" (Luke 20:25). Five or six hours before His death He said to Pilate: "My kingdom is not of this world" (John 18:36). Jesus, then, was a king: He possessed a kingdom; He had followers; and He desired all men, without exception, to become His followers for the sake of their own souls. It is evident, then, that Jesus intended to establish, and actually did establish, a religious organization—in other words, a church, for a church is nothing more than an organization of persons professing the same religious belief and worshiping God in the same way under the authority of religious superiors.

HIS CHURCH WAS TO ENDURE.

First of all, it is most reasonable to suppose that Jesus Christ would establish a permanent organization, for without it the truths which He came to teach would soon be confused, obscured, or even forgotten. Again, He declared that baptism and Communion were essential to salvation; but how could such sacraments be administered without a priesthood, and how could there be a priesthood without a church to select and ordain the priests? But we need not speculate on the matter, for Jesus Christ Himself declared in very solemn words: "Upon this rock I will build My Church, and the gates of hell shall not prevail against it" (Matthew 16:18).

THE POWERS OF THE CHURCH.

The powers of the Church were to be threefold. First, it was to teach: "Going, therefore, teach ye all nations . . . teaching them to observe all things whatsoever I have commanded you" (Matthew 28:19-20). Secondly, it was to sanctify. The Church was to give to the faithful the Sacrament of the Altar—for Jesus said: "Do this for a commemoration of Me" (Luke 22:19)—and the Sacrament would be the life of their souls: "He that eateth My flesh and drinketh My blood, hath everlasting life" (John 6:55). The Church was to baptize, and baptism was to be essential to salvation: "He that believeth and is baptized, shall be saved" (Mark 16:16). The Church was also to forgive sins: "Whose sins you shall forgive, they are forgiven them" (John 20:23). Finally, the Church had power to legislate: "He that re-

ceiveth whomsoever I send, receiveth Me" (John 13:20);
"Whatsoever you shall bind upon earth shall be bound also
in heaven" (Matthew 18:18); "I will give to thee the keys
of the kingdom of heaven" (Matthew 16:19).

THE HEADSHIP OF THE CHURCH. Every organization must have a head, and Jesus had said to Peter: "Thou
art Peter, and upon this rock I will build My Church"
(Matthew 16:18). And later, after His resurrection, He confirmed this promise in the presence of the other apostles
when He said: "Feed My lambs . . . Feed My sheep"
(John 21:16-17).

THE PERMANENCY OF THE CHURCH. We see,
then, that Jesus, before leaving this world for heaven, had
made all the necessary preparations. He had selected and
instructed apostles who were to continue His work. He had
told them what they were to teach, and what they were to
do in order to bring grace to men's souls. He had given them
His own authority, making it clear, however, that this authority was restricted to the spiritual realm. About to depart
from this world, He confirmed again His commission to teach
all men, adding a promise indicating that His Church was
to endure forever: "Behold I am with you all days, even to
the consummation of the world" (Matthew 28:20).

This is what the historical record says about the plans
and intentions of Jesus Christ. Anyone who denies that He
established an organized Church, a Church with a head, a
Church that was to continue forever, is accepting those por-
tions of the historical record that suit his fancy and rejecting
those that do not suit his fancy.

JESUS CHRIST FOUNDED A CHURCH

POINTS FOR REVIEW AND DISCUSSION

1. Why was it not absolutely necessary for Jesus Christ to establish a Church?

2. Show that He did establish a permanent Church with power to teach, sanctify, and rule.

3. Show that the Church has a divinely appointed head.

4. Walter Lippmann writes as follows:

"It is significant that Jesus was content to leave the governance of the mass of men to Caesar, and that he created no organization during his lifetime beyond the appointment of the Apostles. It is significant, because it shows how much more he was concerned with the few who could be saved than with arranging the affairs of the mass of mankind."

   a. To what extent did Jesus "leave the governance of the mass of men to Caesar"?

   b. Was the appointment of the apostles, correctly understood, all the organization that was necessary?

   c. Is there any evidence that Jesus thought only a few could be saved?

   d. Which "affairs of mankind" did Jesus desire to "arrange"? Can you quote any of His own words to show that He desired to arrange them quite completely?

THE NEXT LESSON

In the next lesson we will study the Gospel record for the purpose of determining still more definitely who the head of Christ's Church was to be, and what powers he was to enjoy.

CHAPTER THIRTY-FIVE

THE AUTHORITY OF ST. PETER

**HE IMPORTANCE OF THE QUESTION.** We have seen in the last lesson that Christ founded a permanent society, a Church, of which He made St. Peter the head. It is important to establish this last point somewhat more fully, for the Catholic Church has always claimed that its supreme pontiffs, the popes, were the legitimate successors of St. Peter. If St. Peter was not the head of the Church, then the present pope and all other popes have made false claims, for they have appealed to the authority possessed by St. Peter as a proof of their own authority. Let us, then, examine more closely into the position of St. Peter both before and after the ascension of Christ into heaven.

JESUS ALWAYS SHOWED ST. PETER SPECIAL HONOR. In many ways St. Peter had from the beginning a position different from that of the other apostles. It appears from three of the evangelists (Matthew 8:14, Mark

1:29, Luke 4:38) that Jesus was accustomed to stay at Peter's home during His public life. In more than one place St. Peter is represented as the leader among the apostles; St. Mark, for example, tells us that, when Jesus went into the desert to pray, "Simon and they that were with him followed after Him" (Mark 1:36). When Caesar's tax collectors came, Jesus did not pay the tax or tribute for all the apostles, but He did send St. Peter to the sea to take from the fish the miraculous coin, telling him to "give it to them for Me and thee" (Matthew 17:26). The other apostles apparently interpreted this as another indication that St. Peter was to outrank them in Christ's kingdom, for they immediately began to ask Christ who was to be the first (Matthew 18:1). And after Christ's resurrection the angels sent a special message to St. Peter by the holy women (Mark 16:7), St. John out of respect waited for St. Peter to go first into the empty sepulcher (John 20:5), and finally Christ appeared to St. Peter alone, as we read in St. Luke: "The Lord is risen indeed and hath appeared to Simon" (Luke 24:34).

JESUS MADE ST. PETER THE HEAD OF HIS CHURCH. All this shows the peculiar position which St. Peter held among the apostles, but it is not the real proof for the fact that Jesus made him the head of the Church. The proof for the headship of St. Peter is taken from the words of Christ Himself—words uttered in a solemn manner, under solemn circumstances, and in the presence of the disciples: "Thou art Peter, and upon this rock I will build My Church, and the gates of hell shall not prevail against it. And I will give to thee the keys of the kingdom of heaven. And whatsoever thou shalt bind upon earth, it shall be bound also in heaven; and whatsoever thou shalt loose on earth, it shall be loosed also in heaven" (Matthew 16:18-19). And this promise was confirmed when, after His resurrection, Jesus entrusted to Peter the flock which He Himself was about to leave (John 21:15-17).

Those who do not wish to recognize the supreme authority of the successors of St. Peter have attempted to explain these words in many different ways, many of them fantastic and far-fetched. But how could words have been more clear and simple? St. Peter was to be the rock on which the Church was built; he was to have possession of the keys of the kingdom of heaven; when he said that men were obliged to do a certain thing, God would consider them obliged, and when he left them free, God would consider them free. If you had been St. Peter and had heard these words addressed to you, would you have thought you were to be the head of the Church or not? And if Christ did not intend to make St. Peter the head of the Church, precisely what was He endeavoring to tell him in these very solemn words? Surely Christ, the Son of God, had some intention concerning the manner in which His Church, founded at the cost of His own life, was to be ruled. If He did not wish it to be ruled by one man, why did He use words which it is almost impossible to explain in any other sense? Can we believe that Christ would so mislead men?

ST. PETER ACCEPTED THE HEADSHIP. But what did St. Peter himself think? Scarcely had Christ as-

"And I will give to thee the keys of the kingdom of heaven. . . . And whatsoever thou shalt bind upon earth, it shall be bound also in heaven; and whatsoever thou shalt loose on earth, it shall be loosed also in heaven"
(Matthew 16:19).

cended into heaven when St. Peter began to appear as the leader and head of the newborn Church. While the disciples were waiting for the coming of the Holy Spirit, it was he who on Pentecost day addressed the Jews and explained what had occurred (Acts 2:14). It was he who presided at the choosing of St. Matthias to take the place of Judas (Acts 1:15). On at least two occasions, when the apostles were arrested by the Jews for preaching Jesus, it was St. Peter who answered in the name of all (Acts 4:8, 5:29). St. Peter was the one who passed sentence on Ananias (Acts 5:3). St. Peter visited all the churches in Judea, Galilee, and Samaria: "And it came to pass that Peter, as he passed through, visiting all, came to the saints who dwelt at Lydda" (Acts 9:32). It was St. Peter who decided that the Gentiles should be admitted to the Church (Acts 10:48), and it was he again who decreed that they should not be required to observe the precepts of the Jewish law (Acts 15:7-12).

ST. PETER'S HEADSHIP WAS RECOGNIZED BY OTHERS. We do not read of any discussion among the apostles as to who should be the head of the Church after the coming of the Holy Ghost. St. Peter quietly assumed this position, and the others recognized his right to it. St. Matthew, in giving the names of the apostles, says: "The first, Simon who is called Peter" (Matthew 10:2). But St. Peter was not the first who was called to the apostolate, for St. Andrew and another disciple of St. John the Baptist were called before him, and it was St. Andrew who found St. Peter and brought him to Jesus (John 1:35-42). If, then, St. Peter was not the first in *time,* he must have

been the first in *dignity*. St. Paul after his conversion went
to see St. Peter and "tarried with him fifteen days" (Galatians 1:18). He says also that the task of preaching the
Gospel to the Jews was entrusted to St. Peter, not in the
sense that other apostles did not preach to them, but very
evidently in the sense that St. Peter was their head.

Four of the apostles wrote letters to the people in their
churches, and in these letters we find them speaking with
authority and reproving those who had gone astray. This
was right, for Christ had chosen them all to preach the
Gospel. Why did not St. Peter write similar letters to the
other apostles, showing his authority? Because there was no
occasion for such action; they had all been filled with the
Holy Ghost and confirmed in the grace of God. Moreover,
he could never forget how he had denied the Master, and
was humble in the exercise of his great dignity. He observed the rule he laid down for bishops, not to lord it over
the clergy (II Peter 5:3). When St. Peter, then, was in the
midst of the other apostles, we might expect to find him
yielding the first place to others and refraining from any
assertion of his authority. Never, indeed, does he act in an
autocratic and overbearing manner, but he is always the
head. He accepts, and the others recognize, the heavy responsibility placed upon him by Christ: "Feed My lambs
. . . Feed My sheep" (John 21:16-17). The historical record shows that St. Peter was the authoritative head of the
Church.

POINTS FOR REVIEW AND DISCUSSION

1. What connection is there between the claims of the present pope and the position of St. Peter in the early Church?

2. Give some facts indicating that St. Peter always occupied a unique position among the apostles.

3. Analyze the promise made by Christ to St. Peter and tell what it indicates.

4. Show that St. Peter acted as head of the Church.

5. Show that his headship was recognized.

6. Discuss what St. Peter says of St. Paul in his Second Epistle 3:15-16.

7. Tell what is true and what is false in this statement, which represents the point of view of many modern Protestants:

"Jesus Christ was an uneducated man of the lower classes who possessed a naturally pious nature and an intense love for the poor. His early followers were as incapable as He of founding a permanent organization. Paul is the one who put order into the crude concepts of this little group and became the real founder of Christianity."

THE NEXT LESSON

If St. Peter was the head of the Church during his lifetime, who was to be head after his death? This question will be considered next.

CHAPTER THIRTY-SIX

THE SUCCESSORS OF
ST. PETER

UCCESSORS TO ST. PETER MUST EXIST. We have shown (1) that Christ established a Church, (2) that He intended this Church to exist until the end of time, and (3) that He made St. Peter the head of this Church. If this is the case, it is evident that, when St. Peter died, someone else must have succeeded to the position which he left vacant. For when Christ said that St. Peter was to be the rock upon which the Church rested, He did not mean that this rock, this principle of unity, order, and strength, would cease to exist when St. Peter died. On the contrary, He promised that it would exist forever; He said: "The gates of hell shall not prevail against it" (Matthew 16:18). So we see that it was Christ's intention that St. Peter should have successors possessed of his authority. It follows from this that there must exist in the world today some man who is the true successor of St. Peter, some man who has authority over all the members of the Church, some man with

power to say what is true or false, what is right or wrong in matters connected with the worship of God and the salvation of our souls. Who and where is this man?

THE ROMAN PONTIFF IS THE SUCCESSOR OF ST. PETER.

There are seven historical proofs for the supremacy of the Roman pontiffs, and they are as follows:

1. The very earliest historical testimony shows that the bishop of Rome was looked upon as the lawful successor of St. Peter. St. Ignatius the Martyr, who died about the year 117, says that it is to Rome we must come whenever there is a question of what the true faith is. St. Irenaeus, who died in the year 202, says that the entire Church depends upon the Church of Rome because of its supreme authority. And just as the English have lists of their kings and we have lists of our presidents, so there are many very old lists which give the names of the heads of the Church; and in every one of these lists the name of St. Peter comes first, and after it come the names of bishops of Rome who succeeded him in office.

2. The bishops of Rome always claimed to have supreme authority over the Church. St. John the apostle wrote in his Apocalypse (1:4) to the seven churches of Asia to exhort and reprimand them; but St. Clement, the fourth pope, wrote to the church of Corinth while St. John was still alive, and wrote in such a way as to indicate very clearly that he considered himself to possess supreme authority. He did not hesitate to act as the head of a local church which was under the immediate control of one of the twelve apostles. Pope St. Victor, who died in 198, threatened to excommunicate

the bishops of Asia. Pope St. Zephyrinus, who died in 217, actually did excommunicate certain heretics who lived far away from the city of Rome. And so we could continue down through the centuries, showing how at all times the Roman pontiffs claimed authority over the entire Church.

3. The Fathers of the Church are those great and holy men who taught the early Christians by word of mouth or in writing. The most ancient records show that they recognized the supreme authority of the bishop of Rome. One of those who wrote most frequently on this subject was St. Cyprian, who died in the year 258.

4. The earliest councils of the Church recognized the authority of the Roman pontiff. The Council of Ephesus, held in 431, referred to the reigning pope, St. Celestine, as 'our holy father' and accepted his decision that Nestorius should be condemned as a heretic. The Council of Chalcedon, held in 451, declared that the pope was their head and that they were his children.

5. Whenever men were in need of an authoritative decision concerning matters of faith, they went to see the Roman pontiff. Thus, St. Polycarp, who died in 155, went to consult Pope St. Anicetus concerning the celebration of Easter, and St. Irenaeus, who died in 202, consulted Pope St. Eleutherius. But, on the other hand, there is no record that any bishop of Rome ever submitted to the opinion or decision of anyone else concerning matters of faith—not because they lacked humility, but simply because of the fact that there did not exist any higher authority to which they could appeal.

6. Ancient Christian art testifies to the supremacy of the Roman pontiff, who is frequently represented in one way or another as the successor of St. Peter and the chief pastor of the flock.

7. Finally, there is one argument which would be sufficient in itself if all other arguments were lacking. It was certainly Christ's intention that His Church should have a head. And nobody can really be the head of the Church unless he knows that he is the head. To be the head of the Church means to have authority over the Church and to exercise that authority for the purpose of preserving the truth which Christ gave to the Church. How can anyone be head of the Church unless he knows that he is the head and unless he acts as the head? But in all the world there is no one except the Roman pontiff, the bishop of Rome, who claims to be the head of the Church. If he is not the head, the Church founded by Christ has no head at all, and His promise has not been fulfilled. Worse than this, the one who claims to be the head—the pope—is an usurper. He claims to possess the right to command all the faithful and to decide what is true and what is false in things pertaining to faith, but he has no more right to do this than you would have to sit in the chair of the chief justice of the Supreme Court and decide cases pertaining to the law of the land. And if the pope is an usurper, if he is telling men and women to do things and to believe things which he has no right to tell them to do or to believe, then the gates of hell have prevailed against the Church. Satan would exult over such a thing as this, for every good man and woman in the

world who is seeking to serve God in the right way as a member of the Catholic Church would be deceiving himself in a matter vitally affecting his eternal salvation.

THE PROOF FROM AUTHORITY. Finally, we know that Christ promised that His Church would always have His assistance in teaching men the truth—in other words, that the Church is infallible. But the Church has made it a matter of faith that the Roman pontiff is the true successor of St. Peter and the head of the Church. It follows that the pope is indeed the chief shepherd of the flock of Christ. He has all those powers of ruling and of teaching which Christ conferred upon St. Peter. When doubts arise as to what we should do in order to serve God and save our souls, we have someone who can answer our questions with absolute certainty. And thus the promise of Christ has been fulfilled: "Upon this rock I will build My Church, and the gates of hell shall not prevail against it" (Matthew 16:18).

POINTS FOR REVIEW AND DISCUSSION

1. Give the proofs for the supremacy of the Roman pontiffs from (1) early historical writings, (2) the belief of the earliest Roman pontiffs, (3) the Fathers of the Church, (4) the early councils, (5) the action of early Christians when in search of authoritative decisions, (6) ancient Christian art, and (7) the failure of anyone else to claim to be the head of the Church.

2. Give the proof for the supremacy of the Roman pontiffs from authority.

3. Answer this argument: "The Roman Church finally succeeded

in gaining possession of supreme authority because it was mor
powerful and aggressive than other churches."

THE NEXT LESSON

We have seen that the Church has the duty of teaching mankin
With what certainty does the Church teach? Is she ever subject t
error, or is she infallible?

CHAPTER THIRTY-SEVEN

THE INFALLIBILITY
OF THE CHURCH

HE CHURCH MUST BE INFALLIBLE. The Latin word *fallor* means *to be deceived, to be wrong,* and *infallible* means *incapable of being wrong,* or *free from the possibility of error.*

A little reflection will show us that the Church of Christ ought to be infallible. For Christ came upon earth for the purpose of establishing an organization which would help men to know and worship God in the right way. If after a few generations or a few centuries this organization was unable to say with certainty what Christ had really taught, if it was teaching things that were false, then the world would be just as badly off as it was before the coming of Christ. And this is precisely the condition in which the Protestant sects find themselves. Very many good men and women among these sects accept and live up to some of the doctrines taught by Christ, and for this reason their lives sometimes put careless Catholics to shame. But they can never be absolutely certain that they are right. Even their clergymen disagree among themselves on very fundamental questions, and it is quite evident that in their case the command of God has not been fully observed, nor His promise fulfilled: "Going, therefore, teach ye all nations . . . teaching them to observe *all things* whatsoever I have commanded you: and behold I am with you all days even to the consummation of the world" (Matthew 28:19-20).

TO WHAT EXTENT IS THE CHURCH INFALLIBLE? The Church is infallible only in matters pertaining to faith and morals. This is evident from the fact that Christ founded the Church for the purpose of helping men to save their souls. He did not found it for the purpose of teaching literature, or mathematics, or science. Hence the Church does not attempt to express an authoritative judgment in matters such as these, except in rare cases when there is a close connection between science and religion. For example, it belongs to the sciences of biology and psychology to discuss the nature of man and the kind of soul which he possesses; but the Church can also speak in this matter, for all her work has to do with the souls of men, and consequently she must know what those souls are like. But in scientific matters which have no connection whatsoever with religion, the Church does not express an authoritative opinion. Sometimes, however, the Church forbids her members to teach certain scientific theories, not because she considers the theories incorrect, but because she sees that they disturb the religious life of her children. For example, you have read some of the plays of Shakespeare, and you probably know that certain scholars believe that these plays were really

written by Francis Bacon. If the Church found that a controversy on a point such as this was preventing her members from serving God as they should, she could oblige them to cease discussing it, just as she can forbid them to engage in any activity which does damage to their souls.

Priests preach from their pulpits to the people, but nobody considers their utterances infallibly true. The bishops of certain countries, such as the United States, meet and address pastoral letters to the Catholics of the entire country, but we do not look upon the contents of these letters as infallibly true. But we do find pronouncements that are infallibly true in five sources. They are as follows:

1. The decrees of ecumenical councils (that is, councils representing the entire world, and not merely a part of the world) which have been approved and confirmed by the pope. If the pope refuses to confirm such decrees, they cannot be true, for the Church can never be right when it is in opposition to its divinely appointed head.

2. The decrees of the pope when he evidently intends to exercise his supreme teaching authority in matters of faith and morals.

3. The unanimous consent of theologians; for if all those who have published books dealing with faith and morals were wrong, it would follow that Christ had failed to preserve His Church from error.

4. The unanimous teaching of bishops and priests scattered throughout the world; for here again, if all of them believed something false, it would be evident that Christ had failed to keep His promise.

5. The unanimous conviction of all the faithful throughout the world, for the same reason as that just given.

IN WHAT MATTERS IS THE CHURCH INFALLIBLE? The Church is infallible, as we have said, in matters pertaining to faith and morals. The Church, therefore, is infallible in the following things:

1. In stating what the revealed truth of God is, and in passing judgment on anything bound up with the truth of God.

2. In passing laws for the government of the faithful; for example, that we must abstain on Fridays, that the clergy must not marry, that Mass can be celebrated only at certain hours, and so forth. These laws need not be the very best and most prudent that could be imagined, but they cannot be positively unwise and harmful, for then the Church would be leading men astray.

3. In approving the constitutions and rules of religious orders. If the Church approved constitutions and rules which were opposed to true piety, she would be causing large numbers of persons to spend their lives in a way not pleasing to God.

4. In canonizing saints, for when the Church canonizes a saint, she proposes him to our imitation. But when the Church canonizes a saint, she puts her seal of approval only on the virtues of the saint; she does not express any opinion concerning his wisdom or his ability in purely worldly matters.

THE CHURCH AND NEW TRUTH. The Church does not invent new truths; she merely teaches, explains, and interprets the truth revealed by Christ to and through the apostles. In the course of time new dogmas are proclaimed, but they are new only in the sense that some truth which was always held by the Church is more fully, clearly, and authoritatively expressed. But has not God made new revelations through some of the saints—for example, through St. Margaret Mary? We may believe that He has, but these revelations are far different from the revelations made to the apostles. They are helpful, comforting, instructive, and pious, but we are not obliged to believe them under pain of becoming heretics. The Church maintains that all those truths which every Catholic is absolutely bound to believe were revealed by God before the death of the last of the apostles. To doubt the revelations made to St. Margaret Mary Alacoque or St. Bernadette Soubirous might be rash and irreverent, but it could never be heretical.

THE PLACE OF TRADITION. Christ did not tell His apostles to go forth and *write;* He told them to go forth and *preach.* His Church is a *living* authority which uses, but does not exclusively depend upon, the written record. We can find Christ's truth in printed books, but if all books were destroyed, the Church would still remain in possession of the truth. The early Christians had no written record before the Gospels were composed. Later, the wicked emperor Diocletian ordered all the books of the Christians destroyed, and so many were burned that it is remarkable that we have any record at all of those early days. Written books are not the only source upon which the Church depends; another source is *tradition,* which is the daily teaching of the universal Church as handed down from generation to generation.

This, then, is the meaning of the infallibility of the Church. Christ promised this infallibility to His Church, and therefore one way of quickly identifying the Church founded by Christ is to search for one which claims infallibility. Of all Christian churches, only the Catholic Church makes this claim. Some years ago two zealous Episcopalian clergymen were discussing the sacrament of confirmation. One of them said that he considered it a true sacrament through which grace was conferred. The other said that he did not look upon it as a sacrament, but rather as a sort of initiation ceremony by which young people were introduced to the adult life of the congregation. So, likewise, some Protestants believe that Christ is truly present in the Blessed Sacrament, and others do not. Surely these are matters of vital importance. If we adore the Blessed Sacrament when it should not be adored, we are guilty of idolatry; if we reject it as a sacrament when it is a sacrament, we deprive ourselves of that spiritual life which Christ said was essential. Those who refuse to accept any infallible authority are constantly struggling forward in dense darkness without any guide. If Christ had not made His Church infallible, we would wonder why He had failed to do so. But He did not leave us in uncertainty concerning this matter; He commissioned His apostles to teach all nations whatsoever He had commanded them, and to this injunction He added His promise: "Behold, I am with you all days, even to the consummation of the world" (Matthew 28:20).

POINTS FOR REVIEW AND DISCUSSION

1. Define infallibility.
2. Which pronouncements of the Church are infallibly true?
3. In what matters is the Church infallible?
4. What are we to think of private revelations?
5. Does the Church depend exclusively upon written records?
6. Show how infallibility helps the religious life of mankind.
7. Comment on the charge that infallibility hampers the human genius in art, literature, and science.
8. Discuss the following passages from Walter Lippmann:

a. "To be orthodox is to believe in the right doctrines and to follow the ancient rules of living deduced from a divine revelation. The modern man finds that the doctrines do not fit what he believes to be true, and that the rules do not show him how to conduct his life."

b. "There is much in the teaching of all the spiritual leaders of the past which is wholly obsolete to-day, and there is no compulsive authority in any part of their teaching."

9. What answer would you make to the following statement of H. L. Mencken?

"So long as theologians keep within their proper bounds, science has no quarrel with them, for it is no more able to prove that they are wrong than they themselves are able to prove that they are right."

10. George Herbert Betts proposes as a first principle in religious teaching the following proposition:

"What we believe and teach about God should be in accord with accepted knowledge. Religion should keep step with progress in human thought."

a. What is this "accepted knowledge" which has power to make the Church change what she teaches?

b. In a certain sense religion should keep step with progress in human thought. This textbook, for example, might not have been fully satisfactory to St. Patrick or St. Boniface. Why not? And in what way should religion keep step with progress in human thought?

THE NEXT LESSON

The next lesson, the final one of our book, will explain how Jesus, the Redeemer, restored to us our right to supernatural happiness.

CHAPTER THIRTY - EIGHT

THE TWOFOLD LIGHT

**UR PURPOSE ACHIEVED.**
We have now accomplished the work
which we set out to do. We have shown
by clear and solid arguments that God
exists, that man was created to merit everlasting happiness by the religious worship of God, that Jesus
Christ was truly God and truly man, and that He established
an unfailing and infallible Church with power to teach, to
sanctify, and to rule. The light of reason has guided us,
assisted by that divine grace without which we can do
nothing, to the light of faith. We recognize in the Catholic
Church the one religious organization enjoying the fullness
of divine approval and empowered to speak with authority
on religious matters. Now that we know that the Church
founded by Christ is infallible, we can turn to it for an
answer to any question concerning God and our souls.

JESUS CHRIST THE REDEEMER. Before bringing
this book to an end, let us seek from the Church an answer
to one question which has been frequently before our minds.
It is this: Why did God become man and die on the cross?

Why did the human race stand in need of a Redeemer? And in what does redemption consist?

THE SUPERNATURAL ORDER AND ORIGINAL SIN. The answer to this question explains what to others is one of the greatest mysteries of life; namely, why it is that man, the only creature on earth endowed with an intellect, should be so subject to gross passions, so cruel, so proud, so weak, and so incapable of overcoming in a fully satisfactory manner the obstacles to his own peace, contentment, and well-being—obstacles which in so many cases are the product of his own folly.

The surface of the earth is dotted with prisons, hospitals, and asylums for the insane. Newspapers would be reduced to half their size if they omitted all stories of sin, or crime, and of disasters due to human ignorance and folly. What is the matter with the intellect that God gave to man? Did God fail when He designed it? All other creatures do with ease those things for which they are evidently made. Man's intellect was made to reason, and it has far greater difficulty in reasoning well than we would expect to be the case. How does the Church explain this fact?

The Church explains this fact by saying that man at the time of his creation was raised to the supernatural order and that he lost this gift by original sin. By original sin man not only lost his supernatural gifts, but he also incurred certain consequences which are at the root of the evils which we see in the world.

THE NATURAL ORDER. If man had been left in the natural order, he would have lived, both in this life and the next, according to his natural powers. His intellect would have known God only as any finite intellect can know the infinite. Briefly, we may say that man would have known God by reasoning about Him, just as we did in the early pages of this book. This knowledge of God can bring a very great happiness; for we see that holy persons who learn to commune with God can be supremely happy, despite the fact that only a few saints who have enjoyed ecstasies have ever done more than know God as you and I know Him now.

THE SUPERNATURAL ORDER. In the supernatural order man does more than arrive at a knowledge of God by reasoning about Him. He *sees* God. We have heard and spoken so often about 'seeing God face to face.' Have we ever tried to understand what this expression means? How can we explain it?

Perhaps the best way of explaining this is by means of an illustration. Imagine, then, that you were born blind, and that other persons have endeavored by means of words to tell you what colors are like. Think for a moment how you yourself would describe to a blind person the difference between blue and red. Think what words you might use in the effort to describe to a blind person a glorious sunset. It is the same with our knowledge of God as it exists now. What we have is *descriptions* of God. We have not *seen* God. When we do see God, it will be like seeing the sunset after having heard descriptions of it.

Before you could make the rose which sways in the breeze *feel* the delicious coolness of the breeze, you would have to give it a higher power. Before you could make your pet dog or bird *understand* what you are saying, you would have to give it a higher power. Before man becomes capable of *seeing,* and *knowing,* and *apprehending* the infinite God in Himself, he must be given a higher power.

THE 'LIGHT OF GLORY' AND GRACE. What is this higher power? It is what we call the 'light of glory.' The light of glory is a gift which will be given to the souls of those who are saved, and which will make it possible for them to know God in Himself.

But those who are to receive the light of glory after death must be prepared for it during life. They are prepared for it by sanctifying grace, which makes them in a special sense children of God and heirs of heaven. And since it is God's will that the light of glory and all the happiness which results from it should be merited, all of us—except those blessed infants who die before they can lose the sanctifying grace of baptism—must prove our worthiness by retaining sanctifying grace at the cost of sacrifice and trial.

ORIGINAL SIN AND ITS EFFECTS. If we lose sanctifying grace, we lose it for ourselves only. But if Adam and Eve, the first parents of the human race, lost sanctifying grace, they were to lose it for both themselves and all their descendants. God could put this condition upon His gift, for it was a free and undeserved gift. We know the story of the infidelity of our first parents. Sanctifying grace was lost, and with it was lost freedom from death, freedom from pain and suffering, freedom from the unruly assaults of passion, and much of the clearness of intellect and strength of will which Adam and Eve had previously enjoyed.

OUR RESTORATION TO GRACE. Sanctifying grace was lost through an offense against God, and this offense was in a certain sense infinite because it was a defiance of the infinite God. Therefore full and complete satisfaction could be made only by one who was both God and man. God in His wonderful goodness and love decreed that this satisfaction should be made. God Himself was to become man. Jesus Christ, the God-Man, was to regain the gift which we had lost. This is what we understand by the redemption.

But Jesus Christ did far more than restore what had been lost. He showed us in His own person how loving and merciful God is. He left us examples of every virtue. He revealed to us many new truths. By His death on the cross He strengthened us to endure whatever must be endured for the salvation of our souls.

THE CATHOLIC CHURCH THE DISPENSER OF GRACE. And Jesus Christ made the Catholic Church the dispenser of the graces which He had merited. She is the custodian of the seven sacraments; she is the guardian of His revealed truth; she it is who has power to lead us surely and safely to heaven. She is the one broad and unobstructed highway along which we can travel without fear of becoming lost.

It is easy for hostile critics to raise objections against the truth of the Church. You will hear many such objections in the course of your life. Usually no proof is offered—all we are given is an unsupported statement. Very frequently the objection is one which has been answered centuries ago.

In proving the divinity of Christ, we ourselves made an effort to read the Gospel record with an unprejudiced mind and to interpret it according to its obvious sense. All those who interpret it in any other way do one of three things, all of which are incapable of being defended: (1) they claim, without offering any proof, and in contradiction to perfectly reliable evidence, that certain passages were added to the Gospel record at later dates, or (2) they simply deny that words mean what they are evidently intended to mean, or (3) they concentrate their attention on one or a few passages and close their eyes to other passages which cannot be disregarded if a true interpretation is sought.

Let us give one example of this. You have probably observed that St. Paul enjoys much higher favor among Prottestants than does St. Peter. The Episcopalians in particular dedicate many churches to St. Paul, and comparatively few to St. Peter. Among many non-Catholics St. Paul is looked upon as the real founder of Christianity. It is said that he taught many things which Jesus Christ did not teach. Jesus Christ had a message of hope and of love for the lowly poor, but it was St. Paul who made Christianity the religious system which it is today.

Jesus Christ, they say, never referred to original sin; it was St. Paul who introduced this idea, and who treats it in great detail.

At first sight this may look like a real objection, but upon closer inspection we find that it is merely another example of a false interpretation due to failure to study all the evidence.

First of all, St. Paul loved Jesus Christ with his whole heart and soul. He adored Him as God. He laid down his life for Him. His only desire was to preach the gospel as he had received it. He says:

> For I delivered unto you first of all, which I also received: How that Christ died for our sins according to the Scriptures. And that He was buried, and that He rose again the third day, according to the Scriptures. And that He was seen by Cephas, and after that by the eleven. Then was He seen by more than five hundred brethren at once, of whom many remain until this present, and some are fallen asleep. After that He was seen by James, then by all the apostles; and last of all He was seen also by me, as by one born out of due time. For I am the least of the apostles, who am not worthy to be called an apostle because I persecuted the Church of God (I Corinthians 15:3-9).

Modern critics may look upon Jesus Christ as a pious, zealous, but uneducated man with an uplifting message for lowly folk. St. Paul did not look upon Him in this way. To him He was the Lord, the Master—his God. How easy it is to say that St. Paul added to the message of Jesus, but how difficult to prove it!

And in this particular case, is it true that Jesus said nothing about original sin? What did He mean when He said: "I give them life everlasting, and they shall not perish forever" (John 10:28)? What did He mean when He said: "Without Me you can do *nothing*" (John 15:5)? In scores of places Jesus affirms or intimates that without Him we are doomed to death, and that with Him and through Him we can hope for life. What is this death? Not the death of the body, for He did not save us from that. Evidently, then, the death of the soul; and this death of the soul is one which is common to all men, independently of their own merits or demerits. And this is exactly what we mean by original sin.

Go forth, then, into the world prepared to hold fast to your faith and to fight the good fight in the cause of God. Remember that sneers are cheap, and that one with very little true scholarship can make an unproved charge. Your Catholic faith is the one and only body of religious truth which is consistent from beginning to end. If you have not found truth here, you can never hope to find it anywhere.

On a certain occasion Jesus was preaching to the people near the shore of the Lake of Galilee. He had told them of His intention of giving them His own body in the Blessed Sacrament. Among His listeners were many who could not understand a mystery as wonderful as this; they left our Lord and followed Him no longer. Jesus then turned to the apostles, and said to them: "Will you also go away?" Simon Peter, quickly answering in the name of all, replied: "Lord, to whom shall we go? Thou hast the words of eternal life" (John 6:69).

Changes come slowly in the Orient. The shores of the Lake of Galilee are the same today as they were in the time of our Lord. Fishermen, dressed in a fashion similar to that of the fishermen from among whom Jesus recruited the little band who were to change the entire course of civilization, still ply their trade in primitive boats which link the present with the past. Men have changed in many ways, but in essential things they are the same. The onward march of science has not altered man's spiritual destiny, his spiritual needs, or his spiritual difficulties. We cannot believe that God has failed to provide an adequate answer to the problems which vex men throughout the world. Faith and reason alike compel us to that solution which Simon Peter proclaimed in the name of all mankind: "Lord, to whom shall we go? Thou hast the words of eternal life."

INDEX

INDEX

INDEX

Protestantism: agnosticism and, 81; infallibility and, 279, 284; revelation in, 172; sacraments and, 284

Providence of God, 92-97, 101-05

Rationalists, 164-65

Reason: agnosticism and, 76; atheism and, 71; immortality and, 117-21; progress and, 110; purpose of, 89; religion and, 132-33, 139-43, 146-54; revelation and, 165. *See also* Intellect.

Redemption: grace through, 291; necessity of, 288, 291; original sin and, 287-95. *See also* Jesus Christ; Sacraments, the.

Religion: history of, 41-43, 148-54; meaning of, 133; natural. *See* Natural religion; nature of 132-37; necessity of, 138-44; objective, 136; origin of, 146-54; purpose of, 134; reason and, 139-43, 147-54; subjective, 135; supernatural, 164-69. *See also* Catholic Church; God.

Religions, false, 172-76

Resurrection of Christ, 245-50

Revelation: divine, 164-76; false, 172-74, 177; natural, 169; primitive, 260

Roman Catholic Church. *See* Catholic Church.

Rome, bishops of. *See* Popes.

Sacrament of the Altar. *See* Blessed Sacrament.

Sacraments, the: administration of, 263; baptism, 263; Church and, 291; Confirmation, 284; Holy Eucharist, 263; penance, 263; Protestantism and, 284

Salvation: baptism and, 263; Christ's doctrines and, 215; Church and, 273-74; grace and, 290; revelation and, 158

Science: Church and, 129, 280; laws of, 22-31; limitations of, 67; overstressing of, 3; social, 68

Scriptures. *See* Gospels.

Seutonius, 207

Sin: atheism and, 67; free will and, 103; original, 162, 172, 288-94; responsibility for, 103

Smith, Joseph, 172, 174

Social justice, 3-4

Social sciences, 68

Socrates, 160

Soul: creation of, 112-14, 127-28; immortality of, 116-21; independence of, 112; nature of, 107-14, 126; permanency of, 112. *See also* Immortality.

Spencer, Herbert, 63, 76-77

Stoddard, John L., 6, 16-17, 70

Supernatural order, 288-89

Supernatural truths: manifestation of, 168-69; necessity of, 158

Supreme Being. *See* God; Jesus Christ.

Tacitus, 207

Thomas, St., 223, 241, 245, 248

Translations of Gospels, 196-99

Truths: essential, 215; revelation of, 166; supernatural, 158, 168

Universe: design in, 11-20; government of, 22-31; purposes of, 84-85

Victor, Pope St., 274

Vulgate, 198

Wells, H. G., 131, 212, 224, 252

Will. *See* Free will.

Zephyrinus, Pope St., 275